HISTORY'S MYSTERIOUS PEOPLE

INVESTIGATING THE WORLD'S MOST FASCINATING FIGURES

By Arch Stanton

STAR ODYSSEY PRESS

Published By Star Odyssey Press

Copyright © 2023 Arch Stanton

ISBN-9798867348830

Cover design by: Arch Stanton

Printed in the United States of America

(ONTENTS

Part 1: Historical Figures Shrouded In Legend

Caligula	9
King Charles VI	14
Kaspar Hauser	18
The Princes in the Tower	22
William Tell	27
Ned Ludd	31
Musashi Miyamoto	35
Rasputin	39
Blackbeard	44

Part 2: Wizards, Masterminds, Mystics

Diogenes	49
Joseph Smith	53
L. Ron Hubbard	58
Nostradamus	62
Ramanujan	67

Einstein												71

Jiddu Krishnamurti										76

Fulcanelli											80

Part 3: Paranormal & Otherworldly Encounters

Barney and Betty Hill									85

Travis Walton										90

Ed and Lorraine Warren									95

Edgar Cayce											99

Uri Geller											103

Bob Lazar											107

Joseph McMoneagle									111

Part 4: Unexplained Abilities, Survivors, Tricksters, Disappearances

The Wild Child of Aveyron								117

St. Joseph of Cupertino									121

Gil Perez											125

Tarrare											130

Phineas Gage										134

Bobby Dunbar										138

Prahlad Jani										143

Wolf Messing   148

Tibetan Tummo Monks   152

Ngoc Thai   156

Kevin Richardson   161

Wim Hof   165

Tim Cridland   169

Mehran Karimi Nasseri   174

Carlos Kaiser   178

Frank Abagnale Jr.   183

Afterword   **188**

5

Introduction

Welcome, young investigators, to the fascinating world of *History's Mysterious People!*

Have you ever wanted to make your life extraordinary? To lead a life of intrigue, mystery, and legendary adventure? If so, then let these 40 mystical real-life figures be your inspiration! Would you like to wander through the corridors of time, leaving behind puzzles that bewitch the mind? If the answer is yes, then this book is your gateway to the extraordinary!

History's Mysterious People invites you on a thrilling exploration through the lives of 40 of the most puzzling individuals in history! Our journey begins in ancient Rome with the perplexing Emperor Caligula, whose reign was marked by madness and mystery. We then travel through time to meet King Charles VI, known for his bizarre behavior and the infamous belief that he was made of glass!

As we delve deeper, we'll encounter the 16-year-old orphan Kaspar Hauser, whose appearance in 19th-century Germany sparked endless wonder. And what about the tragic story of the Princes in the Tower, whose disappearance remains one of England's most enduring mysteries?

Your heart will race as we explore the legend of William Tell, the skilled marksman with a mysterious past. And prepare to be intrigued by Ned Ludd, the elusive figure famous for smashing machines during the Industrial Revolution. But that's not all! The legendary samurai Musashi Miyamoto awaits with his unbeaten record in duels, and the dangerous mystic Rasputin, whose influence on the Russian royal family is still discussed today.

We'll sail the high seas with the fearsome pirate Blackbeard and ponder the philosophies of the eccentric Diogenes. The founding of strange new religions will be scrutinized through Joseph Smith and L. Ron Hubbard, while the prophetic visions of Nostradamus will leave you in awe.

The brilliance of mathematical genius Ramanujan and the legendary imagination of Einstein will challenge your mind. And spiritual figures like Jiddu Krishnamurti and St. Joseph of Cupertino, the monk who could fly, will introduce you to the mystical realms of experience.

Our expedition continues with the otherworldly encounters of Barney and Betty Hill, Travis Walton, and the paranormal investigators Ed and Lorraine Warren. The enigmatic Uri Geller and Bob Lazar will challenge your beliefs about the known and the unknown.

So, dear adventurers, let this book be your guide as you embark on a journey through history's shadows. Unravel the secrets, challenge your perceptions, and blaze your trail of discovery. The mysteries of history await, and your adventure starts now!

Part One

Historical Figures
Shrouded in Legend

CALIGULA

Was Caligula truly mad, or was his reputation exaggerated by the people around him?

Did he genuinely believe he was a god, or was that just a play for power and control?

The Roman Empire, with its vast territories, grand arenas, and magnificent feats of engineering, was an awe-inspiring empire that ruled for centuries. Within the timeline of this mighty empire, there were emperors celebrated for being wise and fair, and then there were those remembered for being absolutely terrible!

In the heart of ancient Rome, a child named Gaius Julius Caesar Augustus Germanicus was born. Quite a mouthful, isn't it? Most people just called him Gaius. Little did they know, this child would grow up to be one of the most talked-about emperors in Roman history, famously known as Caligula. But why the nickname? Well, as a toddler, he was often dressed in a mini soldier's outfit, including the tiny boots, or "caligae," worn by Roman soldiers. Hence the nickname "Caligula," which means "little boots."

Young Caligula's childhood wasn't all fun and games in tiny military outfits, though. Spending his earliest years in military camps with his dad, the famed general Germanicus, he was surrounded by soldiers and war. Then tragedy struck. Both his parents died under mysterious circumstances, and some believed they were assassinated by rivals. As an orphan, it's no wonder Caligula developed trust issues.

Fast forward a few years, and Caligula's grand-uncle, Emperor Tiberius, was on the throne. But not for long. After his unexpected death, Caligula, to the surprise of many, became the new emperor of Rome at just 24.

Imagine being handed the keys to the most powerful empire in the world at that age!

Initially, it seemed like Rome had hit the jackpot. Caligula promised to be everything the people wanted. He slashed unfair taxes, released unjustly imprisoned citizens, and even hosted gladiator games, chariot races, and plays for the public's amusement. He was, in the eyes of the Romans, a rockstar emperor. Streets buzzed with chatter about their young, handsome leader. But as the saying goes, "When something seems too good to be true, it probably is."

It wasn't long before Caligula's reign took a dark turn. Some say it was a mysterious illness that changed him, leaving him with severe fever and, perhaps, a touch of madness. Others whispered that maybe he had always been this way, hiding behind a mask of charm. Emerging from his sickness, the emperor began making strange, often brutal decisions. He started eliminating anyone he viewed as a threat, including close friends and advisors. He threw lavish, over-the-top parties while the Roman treasury drained of coins. And then there were the odd personal projects...

Imagine this: Caligula ordered the construction of a floating bridge across the Bay of Baiae, made of ships connected together. Why? Just so he could gallop back and forth across it on his horse! Speaking of horses, he had a favorite one named Incitatus. Rumor had it that he gave this horse a marble home, a collar of precious stones, and even considered making him a consul (a high-ranking official). Whether that's true or just a tall tale, one thing was clear: Caligula's actions were becoming increasingly unpredictable.

As days turned into months and months into years, Caligula's behavior grew even more erratic. Among the strangest of his acts was his claim to be a living god. He demanded that temples be built in his honor, and statues of gods be replaced with his own likeness. Imagine walking into a sacred temple and seeing Caligula's face staring back instead of the gods! It was a shock to the religious sensibilities of many Romans.

It didn't end there. He often dressed up as various gods and demigods, including Hercules, Mercury, and even Venus. He set up a temple to himself and had the high priests make sacrifices in his name. It was an outrageous act, and many believed he was mocking the very gods that Romans worshipped.

With such wild behavior, it's no wonder that Caligula made a fair share of enemies. The Roman elite, senators, and even members of his family began to view him as a danger to the empire. In response, he grew increasingly paranoid. He ordered executions left and right, sometimes on a mere suspicion. Close friends, trusted advisors, and even family members weren't safe from his wrath. Trust became a rare commodity in the imperial palace, replaced by a thick cloud of fear.

Though Caligula seemed unstoppable in his madness, his actions inevitably led to his downfall. The very people who were once thrilled by his ascent to the throne began plotting his end. His extravagant lifestyle and bizarre behavior, combined with his brutality towards the elite, made him many silent enemies.

And in 41 AD, their patience ran out. A group of officers from the Praetorian Guard, the very people sworn to protect the emperor, hatched a plot against him. In the dimly lit underground corridors of the Palatine Games, they cornered and assassinated Caligula, ending the tyrannical reign of one of Rome's most infamous emperors. He was only 28 years old.

In the aftermath of Caligula's death, the Senate attempted a damnatio memoriae, a Latin phrase which means "condemnation of memory." This was an act where Roman officials sought to erase all traces of a person from historical records. All of Caligula's statues were torn down, his coins melted, and his laws undone. Every physical sign of his reign was to be obliterated. The Senate wanted the people to forget him, as if he had never existed. But as history has shown, it's nearly impossible to completely erase someone as unforgettable as Caligula. Despite their best efforts, tales of his wild reign persisted and have been handed down through the ages. His reign serves as a stark reminder of the dangers of unchecked power and the fine line between genius and madness.

Caligula remains, without a doubt, one of history's strangest rulers.

KING CHARLES VI

Why did King Charles VI suddenly believe he was made of glass?

What caused his unpredictable episodes of madness throughout his reign?

Picture this: France, the late 14th century, a nation buzzing with knights, castles, and lavish courts. At the center of it all was a young king, Charles VI, ascending the throne at a mere 11 years old. But as time would reveal, Charles wasn't your average king. No, he had some quirks that would earn him a place in the history books as one of the oddest rulers ever.

Initially, things looked incredibly promising for the young king. Charles was handsome, athletic, and showed great potential. People even called him Charles the Well-Beloved. But as the years rolled on, the pressures of ruling a nation began to weigh on him, and the "Well-Beloved" started to act... well, strangely.

One sunny day, as Charles was enjoying a ride through a forest, a masked figure suddenly leaped out, startling the king and his horse. The mysterious person shouted, "Beware the king! Do not ride any further!" Though the figure quickly disappeared, this event seemed to trigger his first episode of madness.

Not long after, Charles developed an utterly bizarre belief. He became convinced that he was made of glass. Yes, you read that right, GLASS! He thought that with just a slight touch or a minor bump, he could shatter into a million pieces. To prevent this, he had his tailors sew iron rods into his clothing to keep him from "breaking."

As you can imagine, this was a tough situation for France. The nation's leader thought he could break like a wine glass! Charles's episodes of madness weren't constant, but they were unpredictable. Sometimes he recognized the people around him; other times, he looked at his closest friends and family as if they were total strangers. He even once attacked his own brother, not recognizing him and thinking he was an enemy.

Some believed he was cursed, others that he was poisoned, while a few thought it was just the pressure of being a ruler that cracked the king's mind.

If believing he was made of glass wasn't enough, Charles's reign was peppered with other odd episodes. During one winter, the court decided to hold a grand ball. The young king and several of his close friends thought it'd be fun to dress up as wild men, their bodies covered head-to-toe in shaggy costumes. They then danced around, looking like creatures from a forest fairytale. But, as they were dancing close to some torches, a spark flew, setting one of the costumes on fire. Charles was saved, but several of his friends weren't as fortunate. This tragic event became known as the 'Ball of the Burning Men', a dance that turned deadly.

Meanwhile, France faced numerous challenges. From the ongoing Hundred Years' War against England to internal disputes and power struggles, the country needed a strong leader. Unfortunately, with Charles's unpredictable mental state, many took advantage of his condition. Ambitious nobles and even the king's own relatives manipulated him for their gain, leading the kingdom into further turmoil.

But not everyone saw the king as a mere puppet. The common folk, even amidst the chaos, still had a soft spot for Charles. They remembered the early days of his reign, the promise he once held, and many believed that he'd been cursed or bewitched, sympathizing with his plight.

Charles VI's reign lasted for 42 years, but his legacy is undoubtedly overshadowed by his mental struggles. His episodes of madness became more frequent and longer-lasting, and by the end of his life, France was in dire straits. But here's where the story takes another odd turn: On his deathbed, some claimed Charles had a moment of perfect clarity. He allegedly expressed deep sorrow for not being able to serve his nation better and recognized all his family members, even those he hadn't recognized in years.

When he passed away in 1422, France was left to pick up the pieces of a fractured kingdom. His condition, still a mystery to this day, serves as a reminder of the human side of history. Behind every crown, there's a person, and behind every person, there's a story, no matter how strange it may be.

KASPAR HAUSER

Who was Kaspar Hauser really? Could he have been a secret prince, a clever trickster, or just someone who got lost in history?

What really happened when Kaspar Hauser died? Was someone trying to keep him quiet, or was his death just another strange part of his confusing story?

The year was 1828 in the bustling city of Nuremberg, Germany. Among the usual crowd of townsfolk going about their day, a peculiar figure stood out. A teenage boy, wobbling on his feet, clutched a letter in his hand. His clothes were worn out, and he looked bewildered and fascinated by everything around him.

Upon being approached, the boy's words were scarce, as if he could barely speak. He managed to communicate that he wanted to be taken to the captain of the cavalry (soldiers who rode on horseback). But the more the townsfolk interacted with him, the more mysterious he became. His vocabulary seemed limited to a rehearsed script. "I want to be a rider like my father was," he'd repeat, though he couldn't quite say who his father was or where he came from.

Intrigued by this unusual visitor, some kind-hearted residents decided to delve deeper into his story. And what a story it was! According to Kaspar, he had spent most of his life in a darkened cell, isolated from the world. His meals would mysteriously appear every day, and his only companion was a wooden toy horse. He described a life where he never saw the sun, never heard laughter, or even knew that a world existed beyond his small prison.

As you can imagine, the story spread like wildfire. Was he a lost prince? A victim of some cruel experiment? Or simply a boy with a wild imagination?

Speculations swirled. One of the most tantalizing theories was that Kaspar was the rightful heir to the

House of Baden, mysteriously swapped at birth and hidden away to prevent him from claiming his title. But skeptics raised their eyebrows. Was he just a pretender? Someone out to gain wealth and fame?

As days turned into weeks and weeks into months, Kaspar's celebrity status grew. He was not just a curiosity anymore; he was a sensation. Scientists, teachers, and curious onlookers from different parts of the country flocked to see the boy who had appeared out of nowhere. They watched in fascination as he discovered the world, much like a toddler would. Simple pleasures, like tasting fresh fruit for the first time or seeing his reflection in a mirror, left him amazed.

But life as an orphan wasn't easy for Kaspar. While many were genuinely interested in helping him, others saw an opportunity for fame or gain. He changed hands between several guardians, each with their own intentions. Some treated him like a son, while others displayed him like a museum piece.

Yet, amidst all this, a dark cloud loomed. Kaspar, for all his newfound fame, was in danger. He narrowly escaped death multiple times from shadowy assassination attempts. But why? Who wanted him gone? The mystery deepened.

As the narrative unfolds, one can't help but wonder: who really was Kaspar Hauser? His growth under the watchful eyes of Nuremberg's residents was nothing short of remarkable. The boy who had once stumbled upon words was now holding profound conversations, reading, writing, and even playing musical instruments.

He had a particular talent for the piano, its keys ringing with the melodies deep within his heart.

But as his talents flourished, so did the controversies surrounding him. Some suggested that he was a master manipulator, an actor who had concocted a gripping narrative for some hidden agenda. Theories ran wild. Was he truly the lost prince of the House of Baden, or just a clever impostor?

Amidst the web of rumors, one incident stood out—a mysterious stabbing that would eventually claim Kaspar's life. The circumstances surrounding his death were as puzzling as his arrival in Nuremberg. He was found with a deep wound and a cryptic note, written in mirrored writing. Though Kaspar managed to relay some details about the assailant, his account was clouded in confusion and distress.

His tragic end in 1833 left the city in mourning. The boy who had once been their enigma had grown into their own, and his untimely departure left a void. But more than the grief, it was the unsolved riddle of his life that haunted the minds of many. Who had wanted Kaspar dead? Was his death the final act to silence a potentially inconvenient truth?

In the years following, Kaspar's story grew into a legend. Poets, novelists, and playwrights penned their interpretations, each more tragic than the last. His life inspired debates, songs, and even films. His legacy, strangely, was not in the answers he provided, but in the mysteries he left behind.

THE PRINCES IN THE TOWER

What truly happened to the young Princes in
the Tower, Edward V and his brother, Richard?

Were they victims of a plot to keep them from
power, and if so, who was the mastermind
behind their disappearance?

In the heart of medieval London stood the Tower of London, a fortress with towering stone walls that served many roles over the centuries. It was a royal palace, a prison for high-profile captives, an armory, and even a treasury that safeguarded the Crown Jewels. The Tower's history is interwoven with that of England itself, and perhaps no story is more haunting than the Princes in the Tower.

As the sun began its descent one evening in the summer of 1483, two young boys, Edward and Richard, were led into the Tower of London. They were not just any children; they were royalty. Edward, at a mere 12 years of age, was the newly proclaimed King Edward V, and Richard, his younger brother, was the Duke of York. The reason for their stay at the Tower? To supposedly prepare Edward for his coronation as the King of England.

To the onlookers, it might have seemed like a routine affair, a temporary lodging before the grand ceremony. But as days turned to weeks and weeks into months, the two princes were seen less and less, their playful laughter no longer echoing through the Tower's cold halls. Rumors began to circulate of foul play, and soon, the two young royals vanished entirely.

The story of the Princes in the Tower reads like a dramatic play, filled with ambitious characters and twisted plots. Their father, King Edward IV, had died unexpectedly, leaving his eldest son, Edward, as the rightful heir. But in the power-hungry world of medieval England, a child king was seen by many as an opportunity. An opportunity to control, manipulate, and further personal ambitions.

One such figure was the princes' uncle, Richard, the Duke of Gloucester. As the Lord Protector, he was responsible for the young king's safety and the governance of the realm until Edward came of age. But soon after the princes' disappearance, Richard took the throne for himself, becoming King Richard III. This swift power grab raised many eyebrows. Was the ambitious uncle involved in the princes' mysterious disappearance? Or were there other dark forces at play?

The people were divided. Many felt that the uncle, jealous of his nephews, had them removed. However, evidence was scarce. No one had seen the act, no bodies were found, and no confessions were made. The princes, it seemed, had vanished into thin air.

For the teenagers of England, the tale was both cautionary and captivating. Late-night fireside chats would often turn to hushed discussions about the princes. What could life have been like for two young royals, confined within the stone walls of the Tower? Were they lonely, scared, hopeful for a return to the outside world? And the most chilling of questions – were they still alive?

With every passing year, the absence of the two princes from the public eye became more palpable. The Tower's grim reputation only fueled the speculation. After all, it was not just a royal residence; it had seen countless prisoners and many executions. The Tower, for all its might and majesty, also held the power to silence those who posed a threat.

Historians and scholars have combed through records, letters, and testimonies of the time, hoping to find some clue, some indication of what might have befallen the princes. Some theories suggest that they were smuggled out of the Tower and lived the rest of their days in secrecy. Others, more sinister in nature, propose that the boys were murdered in their sleep, their bodies buried deep within the walls or foundations of the Tower, forever silenced by someone who desired the throne.

As the reign of King Richard III progressed, he faced rebellions and unrest, fueled by rumors of his involvement in his nephews' disappearance. Barely two years after his coronation, Richard was killed at the Battle of Bosworth Field, marking the end of the Wars of the Roses and the rise of the Tudor dynasty.

Henry VII, the first Tudor king, had his own reasons for letting the mystery of the princes' fate remain unsolved. Any definitive proof of their deaths could potentially threaten his claim to the throne. Thus, the disappearance of the Princes in the Tower became a political tool, a shadowy tale wielded by those in power to further their own ends.

For the common people, the story of the lost princes was a tragic reminder of the sacrifices made in the ruthless game of thrones. Ballads were composed, tales were spun, and the story was passed down through generations. Even today, the Tower of London, one of

England's most popular tourist destinations, is haunted by their memory. Visitors from all over the world walk its grounds, gazing up at the windows and wondering about the fate of the two young boys who once called it home.

In the years that followed, several pretenders came forth, claiming to be one of the lost princes. While most were dismissed, some gained considerable followings and even posed significant threats to the ruling monarchs. The most famous of these was Perkin Warbeck, who for a time convinced many in Europe that he was Richard, Duke of York. Though eventually captured and executed by Henry VII, his story added another layer to the enduring mystery.

As we close this chapter, we are left with more questions than answers. While we may never know for certain what became of Edward and Richard, their legacy lives on, a reminder of a time when power, politics, and treachery ruled the land.

WILLIAM TELL

Did William Tell, the legendary Swiss marksman, truly exist or is he just a legendary figure?

Did the famed apple-shot moment actually happen or is it a product of creative storytelling?

In the picturesque landscapes of Switzerland, surrounded by mighty alps and serene lakes, people tell a tale of bravery, defiance, and unmatched skill with a bow and arrow. The hero of this story? A simple man named William Tell.

But unlike other heroes who wore crowns or rode dragons, Tell's fame came from one single shot, an arrow that would spark a revolution.

Switzerland in the late 13th and early 14th centuries wasn't the independent country we know today. Instead, it was under the rule of the Habsburg Empire. And like any good story of heroes and villains, our tale has a bad guy—Gessler, a cruel governor appointed by the Habsburgs.

Gessler, hungry for power and control, wanted the Swiss to recognize his authority. So, he placed his hat on top of a pole in the main square of Altdorf and demanded that all the townspeople bow to it as a sign of respect. Kind of weird, right? But this was less about the hat and more about power.

William Tell, being a free-spirited and proud man, walked past the hat and didn't bow. As you can imagine, Gessler wasn't happy about this. Furious at Tell, Gessler thought of a twisted punishment. He had learned of Tell's reputation as an expert marksman and devised a chilling challenge.

Gessler ordered that Tell's young son, Walter, stand at a distance with an apple placed on his head. Tell was given a single shot to hit the apple without harming his son. The stakes? If Tell refused or failed, both he and his son would be executed.

Imagine the tension in that square. The townsfolk watched with bated breath as Tell took a deep breath, positioned his crossbow, and aimed. Time seemed to stand still until the arrow whizzed through the air, striking the apple cleanly off Walter's head, leaving the boy unharmed. The crowd erupted in relief and admiration.

However, Gessler noticed something peculiar. Tell had removed two arrows from his quiver, but he only used one for the shot. Suspicious, Gessler asked Tell the purpose of the second arrow. Tell, being a man of honesty, replied that had he accidentally harmed his son with the first arrow, the second one would have been meant for Gessler.

This bold admission landed Tell in hot water. Gessler, fearing for his life, ordered Tell's arrest. But as stories like this often go, Tell eventually escaped and would later play a key role in a rebellion against the oppressive Habsburg rule.

The tale of William Tell is one of heroism, skill, and defiance against tyranny. But how much of it is true? Was there really a man named William Tell who defied a cruel governor with an impossible shot? Or is this another case where history and legend intertwine, creating a story too captivating to resist?

Now, while the apple-shot incident is the most celebrated aspect of the Tell legend, it's essential to delve a bit deeper. If the story is rooted in some truth, what can it tell us about the times and the spirit of the Swiss people?

In the wake of Tell's daring act and subsequent escape, the legend states that he became a pivotal figure in the fight for Swiss independence. It's said that one cold night, as a storm raged, Tell managed to ambush and eliminate the wicked Gessler, ensuring his place as a hero of the resistance. With their oppressor gone and their spirits buoyed by Tell's actions, the Swiss continued their fight, ultimately leading to the formation of the Swiss Confederation.

To this day, William Tell is regarded as a national hero in Switzerland. But here comes the million-dollar question: How much of this is factual? Historians have been debating the existence of William Tell for centuries. Some argue that he was a real person, a rebel against the Habsburgs, whose deeds became exaggerated over time. Others believe he's a symbolic figure, a representation of Swiss resistance and desire for independence, and that the apple-shot story was borrowed from older legends.

What we do know is that the Swiss pride themselves on their long-standing tradition of independence and democracy. Whether William Tell was real or not, his story perfectly embodies these ideals. It serves as a reminder of the lengths people will go to when fighting for their freedom and rights.

NED LUDD

Did Ned Ludd really exist, or was he just a
myth to rally people against new machines?

What led to the smashing of stocking frames
that started the whole Luddite movement?

Have you ever been frustrated with a gadget or game that just wouldn't work, making you wish you could toss it out the window? Well, back in the early 1800s in England, there were folks who felt that way about machines. And they didn't just want to toss them; they wanted to smash them! At the center of this movement was a name that echoed through the angry cries of protesters: Ned Ludd.

The story goes that, once upon a time in the quiet village of Anstey, just outside of Leicester, a young man named Ned Ludd was fed up. Apprenticed to a weaver, Ned's primary job was working with a stocking frame, a machine used to produce textiles. One day, in a fit of rage, Ned supposedly smashed two of these stocking frames. Why? There are different versions. Some say the frame had ruined his work, others believe he was being taunted or bullied, and yet others think he was just plain angry at the changing times.

Regardless of the reason, this single act of defiance would unknowingly set off a chain of events that would go down in history. Here's where things get interesting. There's no concrete proof that Ned Ludd ever existed! Some believe he was just a made-up figure, an inspiring story to rally the workers. However, whether real or fictional, the name "Ludd" became legendary.

As the years went on and the Industrial Revolution shifted into high gear, more and more machines were being introduced into factories. These machines were efficient and could produce more goods at a faster rate. Sounds great, right? Well, not for everyone. The machines meant that skilled craftsmen were losing their jobs, replaced by machines operated by low-paid, unskilled workers. Unemployment grew, families went hungry, and people became desperate.

It was during these hard times that the tale of Ned Ludd's act of rebellion began to spread. Workers, seeing machines as the enemy, started to band together. They'd sneak into factories at night, smashing up machinery in protest. These groups of rebels began referring to themselves as "Luddites," a name drawn from the legend of Ned Ludd.

One particular night stands out. A group of about 150 men, faces covered in disguise, marched towards a factory. With the rhythmic beat of a drum guiding them and the moon providing the only light, they were on a mission. The factory they targeted was known for its state-of-the-art machines. Breaking in, they went on a destruction spree, rendering the machinery useless. Their message was clear: they were willing to fight for their livelihoods.

Word of the rebellion spread like wildfire. Newspapers covered the stories, and soon, the Luddites became a significant concern for the government. Factory owners began to beef up security, and some even fortified their factories as if preparing for a siege.

The government's reaction to the Luddite uprisings was swift and severe. They saw the destruction of machinery as a direct threat to progress and economic growth. Soon, soldiers were dispatched to the most troubled areas, and many confrontations between the Luddites and the British Army occurred.

Yet, amidst all the chaos, the legend of Ned Ludd grew. Songs were sung about him, stories told, and in a way, he became a symbol of the struggle between man and machine. A popular chant at the time went something like, "Ludd's alive! Ludd will never die! With hammer in hand, to machines, we say goodbye!"

Court trials against accused Luddites were common during this period. Many were found guilty and faced severe penalties, from long prison sentences to transportation to the colonies, and in some cases, even execution. As the years passed, the Luddite movement began to wane. A combination of the army's presence, the severe penalties for being caught, and the gradual acceptance of the Industrial Revolution all contributed to its decline. Yet, the impact of the Luddites and the legend of Ned Ludd were far from forgotten.

Today, the term "Luddite" is still used, though its meaning has evolved. It often refers to someone who opposes new technologies or is hesitant to adopt them. And while the physical act of smashing machines is largely a thing of the past, the sentiment—a wariness of unchecked progress and the loss of human touch—remains relevant in our tech-dominated world.

Musashi Miyamoto

How did Musashi Miyamoto manage to remain undefeated in over 60 duels?

Are the tales of his unparalleled skills and his unique two-sword technique more myth than fact?

Imagine a land where honor is more valuable than gold, where samurai warriors roam, and where each sword clash tells a tale of courage, strategy, and artistry. In this world, one name echoes louder than them all: Musashi Miyamoto.

Born in 1584, in a small village in Japan, Musashi's life was destined to be extraordinary. Orphaned at a young age, the tales say he wielded a sword before most kids could even say their own names. By the age of 13, Musashi had already entered his first duel — and won. This victory set the stage for a lifetime of challenges that would turn him into the most famous samurai ever.

Now, you might be wondering, what's so special about winning a duel? Well, in the era of samurai, duels weren't just about defeating an opponent; they were a dance of skill, a test of strategy, and most importantly, a display of honor.

What's truly astounding is that throughout his life, Musashi fought in over 60 duels, and he remained undefeated. SIXTY! And these weren't friendly sparring matches. They were deadly battles where a single misstep could mean the end. Every swordsman in the land wanted to be the one to defeat the legendary Musashi, but none could best him.

The myths surrounding his techniques are many. The most famous of these is his unique style of fighting with two swords at once, known as "Niten Ichi-ryū". Picture this: while most samurai focused on perfecting their skill with a single blade, Musashi was a whirlwind of steel, wielding both a long sword and a short sword with deadly precision. But was this two-sword style the real secret behind his unbeatable record? Or was it his deep understanding of strategy, which he later penned down in his book, "The Book of Five Rings"?

As Musashi journeyed through Japan, his reputation grew. Tales of his exploits spread far and wide. Legend has it, he once fought off a group of samurai using only a wooden stick, proving that in Musashi's hands, anything could become a lethal weapon. Yet, for all the stories of his martial prowess, Musashi was not just a warrior. He was a philosopher, an artist, and a writer. His works on strategy and philosophy are still read today, offering insights not just into combat, but into life itself.

But like all great legends, separating fact from fiction in Musashi's life can be a challenge. Was he truly the invincible warrior that stories made him out to be? Or was he just an excellent strategist, always staying one step ahead of his rivals? Some believed that his unbeaten streak wasn't due to just his skill with the sword, but also his deep understanding of the human mind. He could read his opponents, predict their moves, and use their own emotions against them.

One of the most mysterious episodes in his life was his legendary duel with Sasaki Kojirō, another famed swordsman of his time. It's said that Musashi arrived late on purpose, infuriating Kojirō. Then, instead of using his traditional weapon, Musashi carved an extra-long sword from an oar and defeated Kojirō with it. Did this really happen, or was it just another legend, a story stretched and shaped by countless retellings?

Despite his warrior image, Musashi also had a softer, introspective side. He was an accomplished painter, sculptor, and calligrapher. His art was much like his fighting style: simple, direct, yet profoundly deep. Some historians believe that Musashi's undefeated record in duels was due not just to his martial skills, but also to his artistic sensibilities. He viewed each duel as a dance, a piece of art, where both opponents were collaborators, creating a story with each swing of their blades.

But as the sun set on Musashi's life, he sought solitude. The once-feared swordsman, who had roamed the lands looking for worthy opponents, retreated to a quiet cave called Reigandō. There, he penned down his life's learnings in "The Book of Five Rings," a text that delved deep into the philosophy of martial arts and life. This wasn't just a manual on how to wield a sword, but also a guide on how to live, face challenges, and find one's purpose.

Musashi Miyamoto passed away in 1645, but his legacy was far from over. His teachings, strategies, and artistry continued to inspire generations. Samurai viewed him as the pinnacle of martial prowess, while thinkers and strategists studied his writings for wisdom.

Today, the tales of Musashi Miyamoto still captivate the world. His life, a blend of fact and fiction, history and legend, remains a testament to the endless pursuit of mastery. Whether through the blade, brush, or pen, Musashi's spirit lives on, reminding us that life is not just about winning battles, but also about understanding oneself and the world around.

RASPUTIN

Was Rasputin truly a holy man with miraculous powers, or just a cunning manipulator?

How did this mysterious figure gain such immense influence over the Russian royal family?

D eep within the snow-covered landscapes of Russia, in a tiny village named Pokrovskoye, was born one of history's most mysterious figures: Grigori Rasputin. With piercing eyes and a wild beard, Rasputin would grow up to influence the fate of an entire nation.

From a young age, there were whispers about Rasputin. Some villagers believed he possessed supernatural abilities, like the power to heal the sick or foresee the future. As he grew older, tales of his mystical abilities spread far and wide, eventually reaching the ears of the Russian royals.

Now, imagine the grandeur of the Russian Imperial Court, with its shimmering golden domes and elegant ballrooms. Here, Rasputin, the uneducated peasant, would become an adviser to Tsar Nicholas II and especially Tsarina Alexandra. But why? How did this man from a humble background find himself amidst the royalty of one of the world's most powerful nations?

The answer lies in a desperate mother's love for her son. Tsarevich Alexei, the young heir to the Russian throne, suffered from hemophilia, a medical condition that prevents blood from clotting. This meant even a minor injury could be fatal for him. The royal family's doctors were clueless, and no treatment seemed to work. Enter Rasputin, who was believed to have miraculous healing abilities.

On one occasion, when Alexei was severely ill and the doctors had given up hope, Rasputin was summoned. He prayed over the boy, and to everyone's astonishment,

Alexei recovered. Whether it was a coincidence, the power of suggestion, or something truly mystical, no one can say for sure. However, from that moment, Tsarina Alexandra was convinced of Rasputin's divine powers and believed him to be their family's protector.

But Rasputin's influence didn't stop at healing. He began weighing in on political matters, offering advice on everything from military strategies to appointments within the church. Many were shocked by his rapid rise in status. After all, he wasn't a statesman or a priest but a man of mysterious origins with no formal education. Whispers and rumors about Rasputin's influence, his wild parties, and his supposed control over the royal family began to circulate.

As his influence grew, so did the number of his enemies. Many nobles and church officials viewed him as a threat to the empire and the Orthodox Church. They whispered about his rumored immoral behavior, his power over the tsarina, and the dire need to put an end to his influence.

And thus, a plot was hatched, leading to one of the most legendary and mysterious events in Rasputin's life: his assassination.

As word of Rasputin's influence spread, anger and resentment brewed in the hearts of many Russian nobles. They saw him as a dangerous manipulator, a threat to the throne, and to Russia itself. Among the conspirators determined to end his influence was Prince Felix Yusupov, a wealthy aristocrat related to the Tsar.

On a bitterly cold night in December 1916, Rasputin was lured to Yusupov's palace in St. Petersburg with the promise of meeting the prince's beautiful wife. The plan was simple yet sinister: poison the mystic and rid Russia of his influence once and for all. In the dimly lit basement of the palace, Yusupov offered Rasputin wine and pastries laced with cyanide. But hours passed, and to the conspirators' astonishment, Rasputin showed no signs of distress. Frustrated and anxious, Yusupov retrieved a revolver and shot Rasputin in the chest. Believing their mission accomplished, the conspirators rejoiced.

A short while later, Yusupov returned to the basement to ensure Rasputin was truly dead. As he approached the body, Rasputin suddenly leaped up, attacking Yusupov with wild fury. Panicking, the prince and his co-conspirators chased the seemingly invincible Rasputin through the palace grounds. Outside, in the snowy courtyard, Rasputin was shot again, this time in the back. Still, he attempted to flee, crawling and fighting off his attackers. The conspirators, determined to end it, beat him and then bound him, finally throwing him into the freezing Neva River. When his body was found days later, there were reports suggesting that he may have still been alive when he hit the water, finally succumbing to the river's icy grip.

The exact details of that fateful night remain shrouded in mystery. How could Rasputin consume poison and survive multiple gunshot wounds? Was he truly as immortal as the legends suggested, or were the stories of that night exaggerated? While we may never know the complete truth, the tales of Rasputin's indomitable spirit have persisted through the decades.

After Rasputin's death, Russia underwent vast political changes. The royal family lost their grip on power, and the Russian Revolution changed the nation forever. The Tsar, Tsarina, and their children, including the young Tsarevich Alexei, met tragic ends. Many believe that the fall of the Romanov dynasty was in part due to their association with Rasputin, the "Mad Monk" who had come to symbolize the excesses and decay of the Russian royal court.

Rasputin's life remains a blend of fact, fiction, and mysticism. Was he a divine prophet, a mere charlatan, or something in between? The tales of his supernatural abilities, his influence over the royal family, and his dramatic end continue to capture the imagination of people all over the world.

BLACKBEARD

What were the true origins and motivations of
the fearsome pirate known as Blackbeard, and
how much of his notorious reputation was
reality versus legend?

Is it possible that Blackbeard's vast treasure
still lies hidden somewhere, waiting to be
discovered?

Imagine the golden age of piracy: majestic ships with billowing sails, distant tropical islands, and seas filled with both danger and adventure. Among the shadows cast by the Caribbean sun, there emerged a figure so fearsome that even the bravest sailors would tremble at the mention of his name. With a thick black beard that seemed to engulf his face, this was Edward Teach—better known as Blackbeard.

But who was the man behind the smoke and legends?

Born around 1680, Edward Teach's early life remains an enigma. Some say he was born in Bristol, England, and had been a respectable sailor before turning to a life of crime. What caused this change of heart? Was it the promise of gold, the thrill of adventure, or a rebellious spirit that couldn't be tamed? The waters of history are murky, but by the early 1700s, Blackbeard was making waves in the Atlantic, becoming the most feared pirate of his time.

He wasn't just known for his fearsome appearance, but also for his cunning mind. Blackbeard was a master of psychological warfare. He knew that his image alone could strike terror into the hearts of his enemies, often leading them to surrender without a fight. This strategy, combined with his undeniable skill with a sword and pistol, made him nearly unstoppable on the seas.

Blackbeard's ship, the Queen Anne's Revenge, became the stuff of legends. Originally a French slave ship, Teach captured it in 1717 and made it his own, equipping it with 40 guns and making it one of the most formidable pirate ships of its day. From its deck,

Blackbeard launched numerous raids, amassing a considerable fortune.

Yet, for all his infamy and treasure, Blackbeard wasn't a mindless brute. Many tales suggest he rarely used violence, preferring to rely on his fearsome reputation. There's even a story that he once blockaded the port of Charleston, South Carolina, not for gold or jewels, but for medicine! Some say he was protecting his crew from disease; others think the medicine was for Blackbeard himself. Could it be that the fearsome pirate had a hidden vulnerability?

Despite his reign of terror...... Blackbeard's career as a pirate was surprisingly short-lived. By 1718, just a few years after his explosive entrance into the world of piracy, the colonies were growing tired of his antics. The governor of Virginia, Alexander Spotswood, decided that Blackbeard's time was up. He dispatched Lieutenant Robert Maynard with a simple mission: hunt down and capture or kill the infamous pirate.

The confrontation between Maynard and Blackbeard was the stuff of legends. Near Ocracoke Island in North Carolina, the two ships clashed in a ferocious battle. Amidst the sound of clashing swords and booming cannons, Blackbeard fought with the ferocity of a cornered animal. Legend has it that he took five gunshot wounds and twenty slashes from swords before finally succumbing. When Maynard later examined Blackbeard's body, he allegedly found a letter from the governor of North Carolina, hinting at secret dealings. Was Blackbeard more connected than anyone realized?

With Blackbeard's death, whispers began to circulate about his buried treasure. Tales of hidden chests filled with gold, jewels, and precious artifacts became the talk of the colonies. Was it buried on a remote island? Sunk beneath the waves? Or had Blackbeard left clues to its location, a puzzle waiting to be solved? To this day, the treasure of Blackbeard remains one of history's greatest unsolved mysteries. Numerous expeditions and treasure hunters have tried to find it, but all have come up empty-handed.

But perhaps the most enduring mystery of all is the man himself. Separating the man from the myth is a daunting task. How much of Blackbeard's fearsome reputation was genuine, and how much was cleverly crafted theater? Was he truly the heartless villain that history painted him to be, or was there more to Edward Teach than met the eye?

In the annals of history, Blackbeard stands as a testament to the power of legends and the allure of the unknown. His story, a blend of fact and fiction, serves as a reminder that sometimes the truth is stranger than any tale, and that the line between hero and villain can be as thin as a cutlass's edge.

PART TWO

WIZARDS
MASTERMINDS
MYSTICS

DIOGENES

Why did Diogenes choose to live inside a tub in the heart of Athens?

How did a man with almost nothing to his name dare to challenge the most powerful figures of his time, including Alexander the Great?

In the bustling city of Athens, a place where great thinkers like Plato and Socrates roamed the streets, there was one philosopher who stood out from the rest. Not because of his wealth or status, but quite the opposite. Diogenes, with wild hair and ragged clothes, made his home inside a tub! While others aimed for luxury and comfort, he embraced simplicity and had the courage to question everything.

Born in a city called Sinope, young Diogenes' life took a sharp turn when he was exiled (kicked out for life). Some say it was because of a problem with money, but like many things in his life, the true reason remains shrouded in mystery. This twist of fate led him to Athens, the heart of intellectual thinking. Here, amidst grand structures and debating philosophers, Diogenes began his unconventional journey.

Upon arriving in Athens, Diogenes became a student of Antisthenes, the founder of a philosophy known as Cynicism. No, not the kind of cynicism where you roll your eyes at everything; this was about living in harmony with nature and rejecting all the unnecessary comforts and fake behaviors of society.

Instead of seeking a cozy home, Diogenes decided on a bold statement. He set up residence in a ceramic tub in the middle of Athens' busy marketplace. People would walk by, their arms filled with shopping bags, and there he'd be, lounging in his tub, observing the world. And when he felt thirsty? He'd drink water using his hands, having thrown away his bowl after seeing a child do the same. To him, if something wasn't necessary, it wasn't worth having.

But don't mistake his simple lifestyle for ignorance. Diogenes had a sharp wit and wasn't afraid to use it. He often criticized the ways of the society around him. Once, he was spotted wandering during daylight with a lantern, and when asked what he was doing, he replied, "I'm searching for an honest man." His antics were humorous, but they also made people stop and think.

One of the most legendary stories from his time in Athens was his interaction with the renowned philosopher Plato. Plato had just provided a fancy definition of a human being as a "featherless bi-ped" (something that walks on two feet). To mock this overly complicated description, Diogenes plucked a chicken and brought it to Plato's Academy, declaring, "Behold! I've brought you a man!" It was his humorous way of showing that sometimes people, even great thinkers, can overcomplicate simple things.

As the days went by, Diogenes' reputation as a fearless philosopher grew. His tub became a spot of attraction, and many came to listen or challenge his views. Yet, amidst his antics and teachings, the day was approaching when he'd meet someone whose very name made the world tremble.

As dawn broke over Athens, an unexpected visitor approached the marketplace where Diogenes lounged in his tub. It was none other than Alexander the Great, the young king who had swiftly carved an empire stretching from Greece to parts of Asia. Tales of Diogenes' wisdom and boldness had reached even his ears, and the mighty ruler was curious to meet him.

As Alexander stood towering before the tub, with his royal guards behind him, the marketplace grew silent. Here was the world's most powerful man, face to face with a philosopher who lived in a tub.

"If there's any favor you'd wish from me, just ask," Alexander said, blocking out the sun as he stood tall over the tub. Many would have jumped at such an offer, asking the king for wealth or power. But Diogenes, without missing a beat, responded, "Yes, there is one thing. Stand out of my sunlight."

Alexander, known for his short temper, paused. Then, breaking into laughter, exclaimed, "If I were not Alexander, I would wish to be Diogenes!"

As the years rolled on, Diogenes continued to be the talk of the town. His antics, while often humorous, always carried deeper meanings. They challenged people to question societal norms and ponder on what truly mattered in life. Despite owning almost nothing, Diogenes was rich in wisdom, and his tub in Athens became a symbol of his philosophy — that happiness didn't lie in material possessions but in understanding oneself.

Today, over two thousand years later, Diogenes' teachings continue to inspire. In a world filled with materialism, his words serve as a reminder that sometimes, less is more. And while most of us wouldn't dream of living in a tub, perhaps there's a lesson to be learned about finding joy in simplicity.

JOSEPH SMITH

How did a young boy with limited education
come to produce the complex and intricate text
of the Book of Mormon?

Did the farmer on whose land the gold plates
were said to have been found truly support
Joseph Smith's claim?

In the early 19th century, in the rural lands of upstate New York, young Joseph Smith claimed to have experienced something so extraordinary that it would change the course of religious history in America. Born in 1805 to a modest farming family, Joseph had the same aspirations and concerns as other boys his age, with one unique difference: he claimed frequent visions and communications with the divine.

One crisp autumn day, while in deep prayer in the woods, Joseph alleged to have been visited by an angel named Moroni. This heavenly being revealed the existence of an ancient record, inscribed on gold plates, buried deep in the ground on a hill called Cumorah. These plates, he was told, contained the religious history of an ancient American civilization.

With a heart pounding with excitement and trepidation, Joseph went to the hill the next day. As he dug deeper into the earth, he soon uncovered a box made of stone. And within? The gold plates, shining brilliantly, bearing engravings in an unfamiliar script. This was not just any script, but 'Reformed Egyptian', a language that, to this day, remains a subject of debate and wonder among scholars.

Now, you'd think that such an extraordinary find would be met with widespread celebration, right? Not quite. Many dismissed Joseph's story as a work of fiction or a delusion. However, there was one significant piece to this puzzle that left even the unbelievers scratching their heads: the support of Martin Harris.

Harris was a well-respected farmer who employed Smith's father. When Joseph shared the story of the plates and even showed him a few characters copied from them, Harris was intrigued. Seeking scientific opinions, he took these characters to scholars, including Charles Anthon, a noted professor of linguistics. To his astonishment, Anthon initially validated the "Egyptian" as being authentic but later seemed to go back on his endorsement, especially once he learned of the story's supernatural origins.

Regardless of the academic debates, what caught everyone's attention was Harris's own transformation. From an initial skeptic, he became one of Joseph Smith's strongest supporters, even mortgaging his farm to fund the publication of the Book of Mormon. It was astounding! Why would a rational farmer, with much to lose, stake his reputation and livelihood on what many called a fantastical tale?

The collaboration between Joseph and Harris was not without its drama. The first manuscript of the translation was lost, leading to tensions between the two. Yet, despite the challenges, the duo persisted in their mission. The Book of Mormon was finally published in 1830, introducing the world to a new scripture and, eventually, a new faith: The Church of Jesus Christ of Latter-day Saints.

But as we turn the pages of history, we're left with those nagging questions: Was Joseph Smith genuinely in touch with the divine? How did a farmer like Martin

Harris become so convinced of the tale that he risked everything?

The publication of the Book of Mormon set the stage for a movement that would soon attract thousands of followers, but it also intensified the controversies surrounding Joseph Smith. As with any tale that toes the line between the supernatural and the ordinary, there were as many believers as there were skeptics.

It wasn't just the discovery of the golden plates that left people in awe and sometimes disbelief; it was the method by which Joseph claimed to translate them. Using the Urim and Thummim, a pair of "seer stones" (stones with holes that he would look through), Joseph said he could interpret the Reformed Egyptian characters on the plates. For many, this miraculous method of translation was a testament to divine intervention, while others saw it as a clever ruse. The plates themselves were shown to only a select few, further fueling both belief and skepticism.

Amidst this whirlwind of acclaim and critique, Joseph and his followers faced mounting persecutions. They were often forced to move from town to town in search of a safe haven where they could practice their beliefs without fear. Each relocation brought with it a set of challenges, but also growth in numbers. Stories of Joseph's revelations and prophecies, and testimonies of miracles and healings, drew people from near and far.

The story of Joseph's life took a drastic turn in Nauvoo, Illinois. Here, he not only oversaw the establishment of a thriving community but also introduced new and radical religious practices. His teachings on polygamy (marrying more than one person) and the nature of God were revolutionary and, to many outsiders, shocking. The tensions escalated, culminating in Joseph's arrest in 1844. While in custody in Carthage Jail, an armed mob stormed the prison, and Joseph, along with his brother Hyrum, met a tragic end.

His passing, however, didn't signal the end of the movement he started. Under the leadership of Brigham Young, the Latter-day Saints embarked on a perilous journey westward, ultimately establishing a new home in the Salt Lake Valley, a testament to their enduring faith and resilience.

Reflecting on Joseph Smith's life, we're confronted with a mosaic of faith, controversy, and mystery. The golden plates, whether you believe in their divine origin or not, symbolize a story that's larger than life. For many, they are a testament to God's continuous revelation to humankind. For others, they remain a far-fetched story. But one thing is clear: the tale of Joseph Smith, the farm boy turned prophet, with his visions, revelations, and the golden plates, has carved an indelible mark on the annals of religious history.

L. Ron Hubbard

What drove Hubbard to transition from science fiction writing to founding a secretive and controversial religion?

Why are the inner teachings of Scientology kept so hidden from both the public and its own members?

Imagine being part of a group where everyone shares a huge secret, one so mysterious that even famous celebrities like Tom Cruise have paid lots of money to discover it. Imagine this secret being guarded so tightly that only those truly committed can find out what it is. That's exactly how it felt to be deep inside the Church of Scientology during its most secretive times.

L. Ron Hubbard, the founder of this group, was not just an ordinary man. Born in 1911 in Tilden, Nebraska, Hubbard was a fiction writer from a young age. Before diving into the world of religion, he was already known as a talented science fiction and adventure story author. With a fierce passion for exploration, he was not only an explorer of lands but also of the mind. He even served as a naval officer during World War II.

But the most interesting part of his story is how he promised his followers secrets about the universe, secrets that could answer life's most challenging questions. Members of Scientology had to go through various stages, almost like levels in a video game. As they progressed, they hoped to gain more wisdom and understanding about themselves and the world. But reaching the top levels wasn't easy; it required time, dedication, and, yes, a lot of money.

It was rumored that at the topmost levels, members would get to know something so unbelievable that it could change the way they saw everything. And remember, even world-famous stars, with all their money and fame, were as eager as anyone else to uncover these secrets.

Outside the Church's walls, curiosity grew. People wondered: What was this grand mystery? Why were some willing to pay fortunes and dedicate their lives to it? Were the whispers about cosmic tales, ancient aliens, and distant planets true?

There's something thrilling about a secret, isn't there? Especially one that's been whispered about, hinted at, and guarded so closely. And for those inside the Church of Scientology, the promise of an unimaginable secret was tantalizing. Remember, they were told they'd discover truths about the universe that most people could only dream of. Some waited years, decades even, to learn this.

Now, let's take a moment to think back about L. Ron Hubbard, the man behind it all. With his wide-brimmed hat and intense gaze, Hubbard wasn't just the founder; he was the storyteller, the visionary. He claimed to have traveled to far-off places and explored hidden realms of the mind.

And here we are, at the edge of the grand revelation.

Imagine the excitement, the anticipation, as dedicated members reached the top level of the Church. They dedicated years of their life, and thousands upon thousands of dollars for this moment. And then, they were told the following secret of the universe:

Long ago, Xenu, a galactic warlord from 75 million years ago, ruled over an interstellar federation of 76 planets, including Earth (then known as "Teegeeack"). To solve his realm's overpopulation issue, Xenu devised a plan. He brought billions of his citizens to Earth in spacecraft resembling airplanes, placed them near volcanoes, and then detonated hydrogen bombs, releasing their souls, or "thetans."

These thetans, Hubbard explained, attached to early humans, passing on traumas and negative experiences. And the goal of Scientology was to rid oneself of these parasitic thetans and achieve a state of "Clear."

To a 13-year-old, or anyone hearing it for the first time, it might sound straight out of a sci-fi novel. But this story wasn't just a tale; it was a fundamental belief for many.

Yet, as wild as this revelation might sound, Hubbard's influence can't be denied. Under his leadership, the Church of Scientology grew into a powerful and wealthy organization. His teachings, books, and courses were disseminated worldwide. He went from a simple boy from Nebraska to a naval officer, a writer, and finally, to the leader of one of the most controversial religious movements of the 20th century.

To this day, many are fascinated by Hubbard. Was he a genius, an opportunistic storyteller, or a mix of both? Whatever the answer, his legacy, and the secrets he shared, continue to be the subject of debate, wonder, and endless curiosity.

Nostradamus

Did Nostradamus truly predict some of history's most significant events, or are his writings just vague verses open to interpretation?

How did Nostradamus create his predictions? Were they visions, educated guesses, or something even more mysterious?

In a dimly lit room, filled with the scent of burning herbs, a man sits hunched over a bowl of water, gazing intently into its depths. The year is 1555, and the man is Michel de Nostredame, better known as Nostradamus. He's not trying to see his own reflection; he's attempting to glimpse the future.

Born in 1503 in the south of France, Nostradamus came from a long line of Jewish doctors and scholars, although his family had converted to Christianity a generation before his birth. Growing up, he was exposed to a mix of science and mysticism. From healing herbs to ancient scriptures, young Nostradamus had an insatiable curiosity, always hungry to learn more.

While he began his career as a doctor, treating victims of the infamous bubonic plague, it wasn't medicine that would make him famous. It was his mysterious book, "Les Prophéties", filled with cryptic four-lined poems or "quatrains" that supposedly predicted the future.

Now, imagine someone telling you they've seen the future, that they've glimpsed events hundreds of years from now. Sounds wild, right? Yet, this is what Nostradamus claimed. His prophecies were not straightforward. They were wrapped in riddles, metaphors, and symbolism. Over the years, many have believed that he predicted major world events: from the rise of Hitler to the 9/11 terrorist attacks.

For instance, one of his quatrains mentions "Hister" and a great war. Some say this points directly to Hitler and World War II. But doubters argue that Nostradamus's writings are so vague they can be twisted to fit almost any event. The debate is endless: was Nostradamus a genuine prophet or just a clever writer whose words are molded to match historical events?

Apart from what he wrote, there's also the question of how he came up with his predictions. Some tales suggest he would sit for hours, maybe even days, in a trance-like state, gazing into a bowl of water or a flame. These sessions, often accompanied by deep meditation or chanting, were said to give him visions of the future. Others think he might have used ancient astrological charts or even secret techniques passed down through his family.

Even within the nobility, many were fascinated by his work. Catherine de' Medici, the queen consort of France, became one of his most ardent admirers. Intrigued by his reputation, she summoned him to Paris for a consultation. Rumor has it that Nostradamus even predicted the futures of her children, though the details of what he told her remain a mystery.

Yet, amidst all the fame and controversy, Nostradamus's personal life was marked by tragedy. He lost his first wife and two children to the plague, an event that deeply affected him. Some believe that these personal losses might have driven him further into the world of mysticism and prophecy, searching for answers in the unseen and the unknown.

As the years went by and his reputation grew, so did the myths surrounding him. Tales of his encounters with other mystics, of secret societies he might have been a part of, and even whispers that he had discovered the secret to eternal life began to circulate.

One of the greatest enigmas surrounding Nostradamus is the manner of his death. It's said that before he passed away in 1566, he predicted the exact day of his demise. When his assistant found him lying dead the next morning, the legend of Nostradamus grew even larger.

Today, his legacy endures. Scholars, historians, and enthusiasts continue to pore over his poems, trying to decipher any hints or clues about the future. Every significant world event brings with it speculations: "Did Nostradamus see this coming?"

Among his numerous quatrains, three that are often cited as his most famous, largely due to their perceived association with major events, are:

The Rise of Hitler:

Quatrain:

"Beasts ferocious with hunger will swim across rivers,
The greater part of the battlefield will be against Hister.
Into a cage of iron will the great one be drawn,
When the child of Germany observes nothing."

Many believe "Hister" refers to Hitler, and the quatrain speaks about World War II and Hitler's aggressive campaigns.

The Great Fire of London (1666):

Quatrain:

"The blood of the just will commit a fault at London,
Burnt through lightning of twenty threes the six:
The ancient lady will fall from her high place,
Several of the same sect will be killed."

The reference to "twenty threes the six" is interpreted by many as the year 1666. The "ancient lady" might symbolize London, and the quatrain seems to allude to the devastating fire that consumed much of the city in that year.

It's important to note that Nostradamus's quatrains are open to interpretation. The connections between the quatrains and the events are made with the benefit of hindsight and can be seen as fitting neatly or seen as vague and general, depending on one's perspective.

Closing the chapter on this intriguing figure, we're left to wonder: Was Nostradamus genuinely gifted with a vision of the future, or was he just a product of his time, weaving together poetic words that would keep people guessing for centuries? The world might never know for sure, but the legend of Nostradamus, the seer of Provence, will undoubtedly live on.

ℛAMANUJAN

How did Ramanujan, with little formal training in mathematics, come up with mathematical theories that continue to baffle and inspire mathematicians?

Ramanujan often said that his formulas were revealed to him in dreams by the Hindu goddess Namagiri. Was this divine inspiration a unique form of intuition, or something else entirely?

The sun hung low over the small town of Kumbakonam in South India. In a modest house, young Srinivasa Ramanujan scribbled furiously in his notebook, lost in a world of numbers and equations. To anyone peeking through the window, it would seem like any other teenager doing his homework. But Ramanujan was no ordinary teenager. He was a self-taught math genius whose talent was yet to be discovered by the world.

Ramanujan's love affair with numbers started early. While other kids played games or flew kites, he was captivated by the world of numbers. By the age of 12, he had already discovered sophisticated theorems on his own. And by 16, he was delving into the world of complex equations, without any guidance or formal education!

But it wasn't all smooth sailing for the young prodigy. Coming from a humble background, Ramanujan faced many challenges. His obsession with math often came at the expense of other subjects. At one point, he even failed his college exams because he neglected all other subjects in favor of mathematics.

Despite these setbacks, his commitment never wavered. He often said his knowledge came to him in dreams, where the Hindu goddess Namagiri would reveal mathematical formulas to him. Upon waking, he'd scribble down whatever he remembered. These dreams led to some of his most groundbreaking work. But were they truly divine visions or just the products of a brilliant mind working overtime?

While his family and friends were in awe of his talent, they also worried about his future. After all, how could someone make a living just by scribbling numbers in a notebook? Little did they know, these scribbles would soon change the course of mathematical history.

One day, determined to share his findings, Ramanujan sent some of his work to mathematicians at Cambridge University in England. Most dismissed his letters, thinking they were the scribblings of a crank. But not all. One mathematician, G. H. Hardy, recognized the genius in Ramanujan's writings. He saw something truly extraordinary, something that couldn't be ignored.

Hardy, struck by the brilliance of this unknown young man from a faraway land, decided to take a chance. He invited Ramanujan to Cambridge. This invitation would mark the beginning of an incredible journey, not just for Ramanujan, but for the world of mathematics itself.

However, moving to England was a big decision. It meant leaving his family, his homeland, and everything he knew behind. But the call of mathematics was too strong. Ramanujan boarded a ship, and with a heart full of dreams and a notebook full of theorems, he set sail for England, ready to dive into the world's most intricate mathematical mysteries.

In the chilly, brick-laden lanes of Cambridge, a world away from the sunny streets of Kumbakonam, Ramanujan stepped into a new chapter of his life. The once isolated young mathematician now found himself amidst the bustling world of academia. He was introduced to theories and concepts he'd never encountered, and yet, his inner talent shone through brilliantly.

Under Hardy's mentorship, Ramanujan's work began to receive the attention it deserved. The pair, despite their differences in background and approach, formed one of the most remarkable partnerships in the history of mathematics. While Hardy was methodical and insisted on rigorous proofs, Ramanujan was intuitive, often arriving at results through intuition and then searching for proofs later.

During this time, Ramanujan's contributions to mathematics were nothing short of revolutionary. From partition theory to modular forms and from q-series to mock theta functions, he dived deep into uncharted territories, leaving behind a legacy that mathematicians would explore for decades to come.

But as the years rolled on, his health deteriorated rapidly. Realizing the seriousness of his condition and longing for home, Ramanujan returned to India in 1919. Back in India, even in fragile health, he continued his work. But fate had other plans. In 1920, at the young age of 32, the world lost its greatest math genius.

Ramanujan's life, though short, left a lasting mark on mathematics. Many of the mysteries he penned down are still being unraveled today, testament to the depth and breadth of his genius.

In the end, Ramanujan's story reminds us that with dedication and love for one's craft, one can overcome even the most insurmountable challenges.

EINSTEIN

Is it true that Einstein was a poor student and struggled in school?

How did a daydream about riding a light beam lead Einstein to one of the most famous equations in history, $E=mc^2$?

Imagine a world where the smartest person wasn't the one acing all their tests or winning school awards. In that world, the genius might be the kid staring out the window, lost in thought, while everyone else scribbles away. That dreamy kid? His name was Albert Einstein.

Albert Einstein, born in 1879 in the city of Ulm in Germany, has become synonymous with the word "genius." Yet, one of the most tantalizing tales about him is that he was a bit of a dud at school. Yep, there's a popular legend that the mastermind who would revolutionize physics was a failure in math. But was he?

Dive into history, and you'll find that this story has been stretched quite a bit. Einstein never failed math. In fact, he was tackling complex algebra by age 12 and geometry the following year. He was the kind of kid who'd devour science and math books just for fun. So why the mix-up? Well, Einstein did face challenges in school, but they weren't about his ability. He often felt out of place, clashing with teachers and resisting strict school rules. His free-thinking spirit didn't mesh well with rigid classrooms. So, the idea he was a "problem student" might have come from his rebellious nature rather than any lack of intelligence.

But school wasn't all gloomy for Einstein. His journey from a curious boy to the physicist who'd turn our understanding of the universe upside down is sprinkled with moments of wonder. One such moment was his fascination with a compass. At age five, young Albert was bedridden due to an illness, and his father brought him a compass. Most kids might have played with it briefly and moved on, but not Einstein. He was mesmerized. The invisible forces that made the needle point north seemed like pure magic to him. That compass sparked a lifelong obsession: to uncover the hidden mysteries of the universe.

Fast forward to his late teens and early twenties. While many of us might daydream about our favorite bands or the latest video game, Einstein's daydreams were a bit... unique. He imagined chasing after a beam of light. What would the world look like if he could race alongside a ray of sunlight? It might sound quirky, but this daydream laid the foundation for his Special Theory of Relativity.

Now, about that famous equation, $E=mc^2$. "E" stands for energy, "m" for mass, and "c" is the speed of light. In simple terms, Einstein proposed that energy and mass are two sides of the same coin. This equation suggested that a tiny amount of mass could be transformed into a huge amount of energy. And this idea was, quite literally, explosive! It paved the way for the development of atomic energy and forever altered the course of history.

But how did Einstein, a young man working in a Swiss patent office, come up with such a revolutionary idea? It wasn't an "aha!" moment that just popped into his head. Instead, it was the result of years of deep thought, imagination, and, yes, lots of math.

While others looked at the universe and accepted the existing rules, Einstein asked, "Why?" Why does time seem to flow at a steady pace? Why can't we catch up to light? By asking these questions and daring to think differently, he crafted theories that transformed how we understand time, space, and everything in between.

Einstein's relentless pursuit of the unknown didn't stop with his early papers and his job at the patent office. He continued to push the boundaries, and in 1915, he published his General Theory of Relativity. This was a radical new way of understanding gravity, not as a force between masses, but as a bending of the fabric of space and time around massive objects. The universe, according to Einstein, was like a vast sheet of rubber: planets and stars warped this cosmic fabric, creating what we feel as gravity.

This theory was put to the test during a solar eclipse in 1919. Scientists observed that the light from stars passing close to the sun during the eclipse was bent, just as Einstein's theory predicted. The news of this successful test made headlines around the world. Albert Einstein, the daydreaming patent clerk, had become an overnight celebrity.

But Einstein's influence went beyond the scientific community; he became a cultural icon. His wild hair and compassionate eyes, his love for music, and his philosophical quotes made him beloved by the public. Yet, for all his newfound fame, Einstein remained humble and dedicated to his work.

Throughout his life, Einstein used his voice for more than just physics. He was an ardent advocate for peace, speaking out against the rise of fascism in Europe, and later, against the proliferation of nuclear weapons. His famous letter to President Franklin D. Roosevelt in 1939, warning of the potential for atomic bombs, played a part in the creation of the Manhattan Project—yet he was deeply troubled by the devastation unleashed at Hiroshima and Nagasaki.

As the years progressed, Einstein continued to search for a unified theory that could explain all the forces of nature in one framework. He spent his later years working on this quest, which he never completed. Even a mind as great as Einstein's couldn't crack every mystery.

Albert Einstein passed away in 1955, leaving behind a legacy that transcended science. He had become a symbol of wisdom and curiosity, a reminder that the universe is a place of wonder waiting to be explored. In classrooms across the world, when a student asks a question that challenges the lesson, they are following in Einstein's footsteps, continuing a journey that began with a five-year-old boy and a compass, reaching ever outward into the vast unknown.

Jiddu Krishnamurti

How did a boy from a small town in India become the chosen "World Teacher" for a global spiritual organization?

What led Krishnamurti to reject organized belief systems and encourage people to explore spirituality on their own terms?

Imagine this: You're 14 years old, usually caught up in the world of algebra problems and video games, and then out of the blue, you're labeled as the "World Teacher." Yes, like suddenly being the main character of an epic story, everyone's eyes are on you, expecting you to lead and enlighten the planet! That's the incredible, head-spinning life of a young boy named Jiddu Krishnamurti.

Now, Krishnamurti wasn't just plucked from obscurity for no reason. In 1909, he was spotted by a fellow named Charles Webster Leadbeater, who was part of a group called the Theosophical Society. Think of this society as a club for people who love to explore deep mysteries of life, blend ideas from different religions, and discuss all things spiritual – sort of like a book club, but for the soul. They were on the lookout for someone super extraordinary, someone who'd help the world see things in a whole new light.

And who was their chosen one? Krishnamurti. Leadbeater believed he saw a radiant aura around him, a glowy signal that this boy was the one they'd been waiting for – kind of like discovering a hidden gem that would soon sparkle for the whole world to see.

Krishnamurti's life took a wild turn, and off he went to England. Picture leaving your friends behind to join a group where you're suddenly the star student in a very exclusive school, training to become a spiritual guide for every corner of the globe. It's intense, right?

While other kids his age might have been learning to ride dirt bikes, Krishnamurti was plunged into the depths of philosophical and spiritual exploration. He found himself at the center of attention, surrounded by adults who eagerly awaited his transformation into the prophesied "World Teacher." But Krishnamurti's journey took an even more extraordinary turn when he began to experience something that he called "the process."

This "process" involved intense, almost unbearable physical pain, particularly in his neck, which was so severe that most people would have sought medical attention. Yet Krishnamurti accepted this pain as a necessary part of a mysterious transformation occurring within him. These episodes were accompanied by profound, transformative insights, altering his perception and understanding of the world. This wasn't just a period of growth; it was a series of life-altering, reality-defying experiences that reshaped his destiny.

Amidst this whirlwind of learning and speaking engagements, Krishnamurti was being prepped for a role of immense spiritual significance. He even had his own group of followers, known as the Order of the Star in the East, all of whom were captivated by his teachings and awaited his emergence as a global spiritual leader. Imagine being a teenager and already having your own fan club, all expecting you to become a guiding light for humanity! But deep down, he was questioning everything he'd been taught. He often felt alone in crowds, even when people were hanging on to his every word. It's like being at the coolest party but feeling like you don't really belong. As he spent more time alone, nature became his classroom, and silence his teacher. He began to see that truth and understanding couldn't be handed down by someone else; they had to be discovered personally.

Finally, in 1929, at a gathering in the Netherlands, Krishnamurti did the unthinkable. He stood up and dissolved the Order of the Star, basically saying, "Thanks, but no thanks," to being the World Teacher. Picture the shock on everyone's faces! He told them that to find truth, you have to be free of all leaders and follow your own path. It was as if he said, "The guide you've been looking for? It's you!"

What came next for Krishnamurti was even more remarkable. He spent the rest of his life traveling the world, not as a proclaimed messiah, but as a friend having a conversation. He wrote books, gave talks, and engaged with people of all ages, sharing his simple yet profound message: the answers we seek are within us.

Krishnamurti never claimed to have all the answers. He didn't want followers; he wanted free thinkers. He encouraged people to question everything, to understand themselves, and in doing so, find their own kind of freedom. It's like he handed everyone a mirror and said, "See for yourself." So, the boy who was once hailed as the "World Teacher" ended up teaching the world something unexpected: that each of us is our own teacher. Krishnamurti's life reminds us that sometimes the greatest mysteries aren't out there in the stars, but deep within our own minds.

ℱULCANELLI

Who was the alchemist known as Fulcanelli?

Did he truly discover the alchemical secret of
the philosopher's stone?

I magine if you could turn your bicycle into a motorcycle just by painting it a different color. Sounds impossible, right? Well, long ago, people believed in a sort of magic science called alchemy. They thought by mixing and melting different things together, they could turn ordinary metals like lead into shiny, precious gold. They also searched for a super special potion called the Elixir of Life, which they hoped would make them live forever. One mysterious guy who many thought had figured it all out was a secretive fellow named Fulcanelli.

In the bustling streets of early 20th-century Paris, filled with clanging trams and vendors selling hot crepes, there was a man who was a bit of a mystery. He was known only by a single name—Fulcanelli—and some say he discovered something incredible. But here's the catch: almost nobody knew who he really was!

Fulcanelli's story is like a detective novel with pages missing. We know he existed because of the two puzzling books he left behind, filled with clues about the lost art of alchemy. But the man himself was as hard to catch as a whisper in the wind. He didn't hang out where you'd expect a famous person to be, and no selfies or snapshots of him exist. It was as if he popped out of thin air, dropped a couple of bombshell books, and vanished, like a ghost who only wanted to borrow a pen.

Let's dive into the life of Fulcanelli through the eyes of someone who actually claimed to know him. This brings us to a young fellow named Eugène Canseliet—think of him as Fulcanelli's biggest fan and student.

Canseliet was just a teen, like a lot of you, when he first met the man who would flip his world upside down. He was dazzled by Fulcanelli's knowledge and his way of making the hardest puzzles seem as easy as tying your shoelaces.

Canseliet would later write about their amazing adventures, like movie scenes filled with strange bottles, smoky experiments, and whispers about changing metals into gold. Fulcanelli's two famous books talked about secrets hiding in plain sight. For example, he suggested that the stunning cathedrals of France were not just places for prayer but were secretly giant books of knowledge. According to Fulcanelli, if you knew how to 'read' the statues and stained glass, they could teach you about alchemy. It was like he was saying, "Hey, these old churches? They're actually guidebooks for turning lead into gold!" And people went wild trying to crack the code.

As Fulcanelli's fame grew, so did the rumors. Some whispered he was hundreds of years old, while others thought he was just a regular guy with a flair for the dramatic. But everyone agreed on one thing: Fulcanelli knew something extraordinary.

But then, one day, as suddenly as he had appeared, Fulcanelli seemed to disappear. Years passed. Then, one last time, Canseliet said he saw his master, and the man hadn't aged at all. This sparked even more rumors. Did Fulcanelli finally make that Elixir of Life? Or did he just decide to live a quiet life away from the spotlight?

His vanishing act left everyone with a galaxy of questions and barely a single answer. Fulcanelli became a legend, a puzzle that begged to be solved, a mystery wrapped in the pages of history.

Despite his disappearance, Fulcanelli's shadow touched many corners of the globe. During World War II, there were whispers that the Nazis were on the hunt for Fulcanelli. They believed the alchemist held the key to supernatural powers that could help them win the war. Luckily, they never found him, or perhaps, he was just a myth after all.

Here's the million-dollar question: Was Fulcanelli a master alchemist who discovered the secrets of immortality and transmutation, or was he a clever mythmaker, enjoying the chaos he stirred? The line between truth and fiction is as thin as a page in one of his books, and that's precisely what makes his story so alluring.

Today, some claim to have seen Fulcanelli in different parts of the world, leading to the belief that he's still out there, wandering the earth, guarding his secrets. Others are sure that the answers are hidden in his writings, waiting for the right pair of eyes to decode them.

So, we're left with a puzzle that's as complex as any video game, only there's no controller, and the cheat codes are in a language we're still learning to speak. But perhaps the real treasure isn't in finding Fulcanelli or turning lead into gold. Maybe it's in the journey, the quest for knowledge, and the thrill of mystery.

Part Three

PARANORMAL AND OTHERWORLDLY ENCOUNTERS

BARNEY AND BETTY HILL

Did Barney and Betty Hill really experience
an alien abduction?

What makes their story one of the most
famous UFO abduction tales in history?

The year was 1961. Rock 'n' roll music was booming, JFK was President, and the space race was in full swing. Yet, in the midst of all these historic events, an ordinary couple from New Hampshire would find themselves at the center of an extraordinary mystery that still baffles many today.

Barney and Betty Hill, a postal worker and a social worker respectively, were not the kind of people you'd expect to be in the spotlight. Their lives were normal, filled with workdays, weekend getaways, and gatherings with friends. But one evening, a road trip back from a vacation in Canada would change everything.

As the story goes, the couple was driving through the White Mountains of New Hampshire. It was late at night, and the winding roads were enveloped in darkness. The only light came from the stars above and the occasional glint from the car's headlights. As they drove, Betty noticed a strange light in the sky. At first, she thought it was just a shooting star. But soon, she realized it was moving in a way no star or airplane would.

Curious and slightly concerned, Betty kept her eyes on the mysterious light. It seemed to be getting closer and was darting around in the night sky, unlike any aircraft they knew of. Barney brushed it off as just another plane or perhaps a military test. But as the minutes ticked by, even he couldn't deny that something bizarre was going on.

Deciding to get a closer look, Barney pulled the car over, and the couple, armed with binoculars, gazed up at the puzzling sight. What they saw next was beyond their wildest imaginations. Through the binoculars, the Hills described seeing an odd, disc-shaped object with multicolored lights and what seemed like windows. And if that wasn't startling enough, they claimed to see figures moving behind those windows!

Panicking, Barney rushed back to the car, convinced they were in danger. The couple sped away, but the strange object seemed to follow them. Their memories of the next few hours were hazy. They recalled hearing beeping sounds and felt a tingling sensation. When they finally arrived home, they were shocked to discover that their journey, which should have taken only a few hours, had lasted much longer. They couldn't account for a chunk of missing time.

The next few days were a blur. The Hills experienced unsettling dreams and feelings of unease. It was as if something profound had occurred, but their minds had blocked it out. The days that followed were filled with questions, anxiety, and an unshakeable feeling that they needed to understand what had happened during those missing hours. Barney and Betty decided to seek help. They reached out to experts and eventually ended up working with Dr. Benjamin Simon, a psychiatrist who specialized in hypnosis.

Under hypnosis, the Hills began to reveal details of their experience, details that they had either forgotten or had been repressed in their memories. Their separate sessions produced eerily similar accounts. They described being taken aboard the strange craft by small beings with distinct features – large, wraparound eyes and grayish skin. Inside the craft, the Hills underwent medical examinations, with the beings taking samples and conducting tests that were unfamiliar to the couple.

But it wasn't just the examination that stood out. Betty, in her sessions, recalled a star map she claimed was shown to her by the beings. This map depicted several stars, some of which were not even known to astronomers at the time. Years later, with advancements in astronomy, the map Betty described appeared to be eerily accurate in representing a set of stars known as the Zeta Reticuli system.

News of the Hills' alleged encounter began to spread. Some were quick to dismiss it as a mere hallucination or a fabricated story. Others, however, felt that the consistent and detailed accounts provided by the couple, combined with their evident distress and the physical evidence (their damaged car, Betty's torn dress), made their story hard to dismiss.

As the years passed, the Hills' story became one of the most famous and debated UFO incidents in history. It opened the doors for countless other stories of alleged abductions and encounters. Books were written, TV shows were produced, and debates raged on about the authenticity of their experience. Throughout it all, Barney and Betty maintained their story. They never sought fame or fortune from their experience; in fact, the intense scrutiny and skepticism often took a toll on their personal lives. Barney passed away in 1969, but Betty continued to discuss their experience and advocate for a more serious study of UFO phenomena until her passing in 2004.

The legacy of Barney and Betty Hill serves as a testament to the enduring human fascination with the unknown. Whether you believe their story or not, it's a tale that prompts us to look up at the stars and wonder: What if? What's out there? And have they, perhaps, come to visit us?

TRAVIS WALTON

Did Travis Walton really experience an alien abduction, or was it all an elaborate hoax?

Why do Walton's story and the accounts of his co-workers align so closely, despite the unbelievable nature of the event?

Picture this: a chilly evening in November 1975, in the Apache-Sitgreaves National Forests of Arizona. The sun had just set, casting long shadows between the towering trees. A group of lumberjacks, tired from their day's work, were driving back home. Among them was 22-year-old Travis Walton.

As they maneuvered their truck along the winding forest roads, Mike Rogers, the driver and Travis's best friend, noticed an unusual glow in the distance. Curious and a bit alarmed, he slowed the vehicle down. That's when they all saw it. Hovering above a clearing was a bright, saucer-shaped object, casting an eerie light on the ground below.

Before anyone could process what they were witnessing, Travis, driven by a mix of curiosity and bravado, jumped out of the truck and sprinted towards the mysterious craft. He later described it as smooth and metallic, with a strange humming sound. Suddenly, a brilliant blue-green beam shot from the craft, hitting Travis squarely in the chest. He was lifted a few feet off the ground and then hurled back with a jolt. Panic ensued among the crew. Thinking their friend was gone or worse, they sped away in sheer terror.

But after driving a short distance, guilt and concern overtook them. They decided to turn back to rescue Travis. However, when they returned to the spot, both Travis and the strange flying object were nowhere to be found. Terrified and confused, the men reported the incident to the local authorities. Of course, the story sounded unbelievable. An alien spaceship in the woods?

A man zapped by a beam of light and then vanishing into thin air? It sounded more like the plot of a science fiction movie than real-life events.

However, the genuine fear and concern displayed by the lumberjacks made the police consider the possibility that they were not just making up a wild story. Searches were conducted, and the area was combed for any sign of Travis or any evidence that could explain his sudden disappearance. Days turned into nights, and there was still no sign of Travis Walton. Just when everyone had nearly given up hope, five days after his mysterious disappearance, Travis reappeared. He was disoriented, weak, and had a bizarre story to tell.

According to Travis, after being hit by the beam of light, he woke up on a sterile table, surrounded by figures not of this world. These beings had large, glossy black eyes, almost almond-shaped, and their skin was smooth and pale. Travis described the environment as cold and clinical, like some sort of examination room. Terrified, he tried to fight them off. He remembered feeling an intense sense of dread by their presence. But at the same time he felt like they were trying to heal him: as if he had been injured by the beam of light and now they were operating on him.

After what felt like hours, he blacked out. The next thing he knew, he was back in Arizona, miles away from where he had initially been taken.

The media storm that followed Travis Walton's reappearance was unlike anything the small town of Snowflake, Arizona, had ever seen. Television crews, journalists, and UFO enthusiasts swarmed the place, all wanting to hear the story firsthand from the man who claimed to have been taken by extraterrestrials. For Travis, reliving the ordeal was traumatic. He suffered from nightmares and became wary of the forest that had once been his workplace. But his story was too significant to ignore. He was invited to talk shows, interviewed by major news outlets, and even took part in documentary films about UFOs.

The small town became divided. Some fully believed in Travis's story, recalling their own strange encounters in the forest or citing the long history of UFO sightings in the region. Others thought it was a well-planned hoax, designed to get attention or make money.

The fact that the entire crew, including Travis, underwent polygraph tests only added more fuel to the fire. The tests, which measure the body's response to certain questions to determine if someone is lying, showed that all of the men were telling the truth about the events of that night. Of course, critics argued that polygraphs are not foolproof and that the tests didn't necessarily prove an alien encounter. Still, the consistent results were certainly intriguing.

Years went by, but the fascination with Travis's story never faded. He even co-authored a book titled "The Walton Experience," which went into detail about his alleged abduction. This book would later inspire a Hollywood film, "Fire in the Sky," bringing Travis's harrowing experience to a broader audience.

As with any event shrouded in mystery, theories abounded. Some believed that Travis had experienced an episode of "missing time," a phenomenon where individuals lose track of time, often linked with alleged alien abductions. Others thought Travis might have encountered a secret government project or experiment. Some even suggested that the whole incident was a hallucination brought on by exhaustion or stress.

For Travis, life after the incident was challenging. He faced ridicule, skepticism, and accusations of lying. But he always stood by his story. The sheer consistency in his recounting, the trauma he displayed, and the backing of his co-workers made it hard to dismiss his narrative outright.

Was he genuinely taken by beings from another world? Or is there another explanation, grounded in earthly possibilities? Until undeniable evidence emerges, the mystery of that chilling November evening in 1975 will continue to captivate imaginations worldwide.

ED AND LORRAINE WARREN

Were the supernatural events they investigated genuinely paranormal, or cleverly crafted hoaxes?

How did they become two of the most famous paranormal investigators in history?

In the quaint town of Monroe, Connecticut, lived a couple who might seem ordinary at first glance. Ed, with his keen detective-like demeanor, and Lorraine, with her gentle and nurturing nature. Yet, when darkness fell and the supernatural world stirred, they stepped into roles that most would run from - they were paranormal investigators.

For decades, Ed and Lorraine Warren explored intriguing cases involving ghostly sightings, mysterious happenings, and houses where people said they felt strange, spooky presences. Of all their adventures, one story really captured people's attention, even making its way into Hollywood movies: The mystery of the Amityville house.

This tale began in 1975 when a family named the Lutzes moved into a house in Amityville, New York. The house, with its beautiful windows, seemed perfect from the outside, but had a troubled history. The year before they moved in, several people had died in the house, a tragedy that the Lutzes knew nothing about.

Not long after they settled into their new home, the Lutzes started noticing odd things. George Lutz would find himself waking up at the same time every night. Certain spots in the house were unusually cold, strange smells appeared out of nowhere, and unseen forces seemed to move around them. Spookiest of all were sightings of a mysterious little girl and glowing red eyes that frightened the family. After enduring these scary experiences for only 28 days, the Lutzes decided they couldn't stay any longer. They left the house, leaving behind many of their belongings, and never returned.

Enter Ed and Lorraine. The Warrens were called in to investigate the supposed haunting. Lorraine, a psychic, immediately sensed that the house had a demonic presence. The energy was so overpowering that during their visit, Ed refused to spend the night. Instead, they decided to hold a séance. Amidst the dim lighting, Lorraine went into a trance, attempting to communicate with the spirits. The session was intense; furniture reportedly moved on its own, and Lorraine was thrown into a whirl of emotions.

This Amityville case drew widespread media attention. Some labeled it a hoax, while others believed every eerie detail. The Warrens, having witnessed the paranormal energy themselves, firmly stood by the Lutzes' claims. The Warrens' involvement with the Amityville house was just one of the many investigations that solidified their reputations as top-tier paranormal experts. However, the Amityville case was particularly divisive. Skeptics pointed out inconsistencies in the Lutzes' stories, and some even suggested that the entire haunting was a clever publicity stunt to capitalize on the tragic history of the house.

Regardless of the controversy, Ed and Lorraine didn't waver. To them, the evidence was clear, especially given Lorraine's personal experiences within the house. Over the years, they would investigate thousands of cases, amassing a collection of haunted artifacts. One of these was a seemingly innocent-looking Raggedy Ann doll, which inspired the famous "Annabelle" movies. According to the Warrens, this doll was no child's plaything—it was believed to be possessed by a demonic spirit.

But with fame came critics. Some accused the Warrens of being sensationalists, exaggerating or even fabricating events for money and attention. Others questioned Lorraine's psychic abilities, considering them as mere tricks to allure the public.

Yet, for every skeptic, there were countless individuals who vouched for the Warrens' authenticity. Families who had once been on the brink of despair due to supernatural disturbances would often express their heartfelt gratitude to the couple. To them, Ed and Lorraine were their last beacon of hope in a world where shadows whispered and unseen forces lurked.

By the end of their careers, Ed and Lorraine had not only created a legacy as paranormal investigators but had also sparked a cultural fascination with the supernatural. Their investigations inspired books, documentaries, and a series of blockbuster movies, making them household names. But beyond the lights and cameras, at the heart of it all, was a simple couple from Connecticut with an unyielding passion for the unknown.

EDGAR CAYCE

How could Edgar Cayce, without any medical
training, provide detailed diagnoses and
treatments while in a trance?

Were Cayce's readings about past lives,
ancient civilizations, and future events genuine
insights or the result of a vivid imagination?

In the early 1900s, when radio shows were the primary source of entertainment and horse-drawn carriages were a common sight, there emerged a man in the United States who baffled many with his extraordinary abilities. This wasn't a magician with fancy tricks up his sleeve or an inventor with a new gadget. This was Edgar Cayce, a humble man with a unique gift that would earn him the title "The Sleeping Prophet."

Born in 1877 in a modest farmhouse in Kentucky, Edgar's childhood was sprinkled with hints of his unusual talents. Legend has it that as a young boy, he could memorize the pages of a book by simply sleeping on it. While this sounds like a dream-come-true for many students, for Edgar, it was just the beginning.

As he grew older, Cayce began to exhibit an even more mysterious ability. He could enter a trance-like state, during which he would provide answers to questions about various topics, from health issues to philosophical inquiries. The most astonishing part? Once awake, Cayce had no memory of the things he'd said.

Imagine being able to solve complex problems in your sleep and then waking up with no recollection of it. It's like acing a test without ever studying for it! But for Edgar, this wasn't a party trick or a way to impress friends. It was a genuine mystery, even to him.

One of the most renowned episodes from his life involves his own health. In his early twenties, Cayce lost his voice and was diagnosed with a form of laryngitis. Doctors were stumped, unable to treat him. But Cayce, in one of his trance states, prescribed a unique remedy.

Following the instructions from his own unconscious self, he regained his voice, astonishing the medical community.

Word of Cayce's talents spread, and soon, people from all over began seeking his insights. They would send letters, visit him, or even telegraph their questions. From a mother concerned about her child's health to entrepreneurs looking for business advice, the range of queries was vast. And each time, Cayce, in his deep trance, would offer detailed responses, often baffling listeners with the accuracy and depth of his knowledge. But not everything was about the present. Cayce often delved into topics like reincarnation, past lives, and prophecies about the future. He spoke of ancient civilizations like Atlantis and made predictions, some of which seemed to come true.

But with fame came challenges. As the news of Cayce's abilities grew, so did the number of skeptics and critics who wanted to disprove him. Scientists and experts from various fields would come to test him, posing difficult questions or trying to catch him off guard. They would examine him while he was in his trance state, checking if there was any foul play involved.

Yet, time and time again, Cayce's readings, as they came to be known, held up to scrutiny. Many of those who initially came as doubters left as believers, astounded by his inexplicable knowledge. While many were focused on the mysticism surrounding Cayce, it's essential to remember he was more than just his psychic abilities. Edgar was a compassionate man who genuinely wanted to help people. Despite the countless demands on his time, he never charged for his readings. Instead, he believed his gift was meant to assist and heal others. That's not to say he didn't face financial challenges. At times, Cayce struggled to make ends meet, juggling his time between his readings and various jobs to support his family.

In the midst of the roaring twenties, a time of jazz, flappers, and rapid change, Cayce established the Association for Research and Enlightenment (A.R.E.) in Virginia Beach. This institution aimed to study spiritual subjects and offer educational programs, and healing based on his readings. Today, the A.R.E. still stands and continues to attract those curious about the mysteries of the mind and spirit.

Edgar's life was not without its personal challenges. His health was often a concern, and the sheer mental and physical exhaustion from the constant readings took a toll on him. Yet, despite these obstacles, Cayce remained dedicated to his mission, providing over 14,000 documented readings throughout his life.

By the time of his passing in 1945, Edgar Cayce had left an indelible mark on history. To some, he was a mystic, a prophet who glimpsed the unseen realms of existence. To others, he remained a puzzle yet to be solved. But for many, especially those he had helped, Edgar Cayce was a ray of hope, proof of the extraordinary potential that lies within us all.

URI GELLER

Was Uri Geller's ability to bend spoons and perform other feats genuine psychic phenomena?

How did Geller become such a global sensation, captivating scientists, celebrities, and even intelligence agencies?

If you ever tried to bend a spoon using just your mind after watching a magic show or a movie, you might just have Uri Geller to thank (or blame) for that little experiment. This mysterious figure from Israel made waves across the globe in the 1970s, claiming he possessed psychic abilities. His alleged powers weren't just limited to bending spoons; Geller claimed he could fix broken watches, read minds, and even see the future.

Uri Geller was born in 1946 in Tel Aviv, which was then part of Palestine. The stories of his mysterious abilities began in his childhood. Legend has it that young Uri was once eating soup when his spoon just randomly bent and broke, with no physical force applied. From that soup-laden moment, his life took a trajectory that no one could've predicted.

Growing up, Geller was just like any other kid, except for the sporadic stories circulating about strange occurrences around him. It wasn't until his early adulthood that these tales took on a life of their own. Geller began performing in small venues, showing off his "psychic" abilities. Word of his talents spread, and soon, he was appearing on television, bending not just spoons, but the collective minds of all who watched.

Scientists, of course, were both intrigued and skeptical. Some believed Geller had uncovered a new realm of the human mind, while others dismissed him as a clever trickster, using sleight-of-hand techniques. But it wasn't just the scientific community that was abuzz with Geller-talk. Celebrities of the time, including the likes of David Bowie and John Lennon, were absolutely fascinated by him. Geller's fame grew exponentially, and he became a household name in many countries.

His rise to stardom was accompanied by plenty of doubters. While performing live on a British television show, he faced a situation where his powers seemed to fail him. The media and skeptics had a field day. Yet, in true Geller fashion, he made a comeback, attributing the failure to external factors and continuing to perform in various venues.

With Uri Geller's celebrity status cemented, the 1980s and 90s saw him taking on a variety of roles, each more unexpected than the last. He transitioned from stage performances to becoming a sought-after talk show guest, offering insights on everything from the nature of the universe to the intricacies of love. While some saw him as a fountain of wisdom, others continued to view him as a fake.

The controversies surrounding Geller extended far beyond heated discussions on talk shows or late-night debates. In the mid-1990s, he became embroiled in a headline-grabbing legal confrontation with Nintendo. Geller claimed that a Pokémon character, "Kadabra," which had psychic abilities, was an unauthorized use of his identity. He asserted that the character's Japanese name, "Yungerer," was derived from his own name and the character's ability to bend spoons mimicked his signature act. This lawsuit wasn't just another tabloid tale; it spurred global conversations about the legitimacy of Geller's psychic claims. From coffee shops in Paris to academic forums in Harvard, and family dinners in

105

Mumbai, the world buzzed with discussions questioning or defending Geller's authenticity.

Books, documentaries, and academic papers continued to explore the phenomenon that was Uri Geller. His life became a subject of study for those interested in the convergence of pop culture, paranormal claims, and the human psyche's vast unknown territories.

But perhaps the most intriguing turn in Geller's journey came when certain declassified documents hinted at his involvement with government intelligence agencies, seemingly confirming earlier rumors. While the extent and nature of his association remained in secrecy, it rekindled interest in Geller's life and abilities.

As his story draws to a close, one can't help but marvel at the life of Uri Geller—a life filled with wonder, controversy, and above all, endless questions. From a simple spoon-bending act in Tel Aviv to global fame and recognition, Geller's journey was anything but ordinary.

In retrospect, whether one believes in Uri Geller's psychic abilities or dismisses them as mere sleight of hand, there's no denying his impact. His story serves as a testament to the power of belief, the allure of the unknown, and the eternal human quest for understanding the mysteries of the universe. And as we ponder on the life of Uri Geller, we are reminded that sometimes, the most intriguing mysteries are the ones that remain unsolved.

Bob Lazar

Did Bob Lazar truly work on reverse-engineering extraterrestrial technology at Area 51's S-4 site?

How did Lazar know about Element 115 years before it was officially recognized?

In the vast desert landscapes of Nevada, there's a place so secret, so guarded, that for a long time, the U.S. government wouldn't even admit it existed. This place, Area 51, became the epicenter of countless conspiracy theories, many of which soared into the public's imagination in the late 1980s. And the man responsible for igniting this wave of curiosity? Bob Lazar.

Born in 1959, Bob Lazar grew up in a world fascinated by space and the wonders of the universe. As a child, he was curious, always taking things apart to understand how they worked. This early passion for mechanics and science led him to pursue studies in physics and electronic technology.

Fast-forward to the 1980s, Bob claimed to have been hired to work in a section of Area 51 known as S-4. Here, he said, was where the U.S. government housed captured UFOs and flying saucers. Lazar's main role? Reverse-engineering the propulsion systems of these otherworldly crafts.

Imagine for a moment being in Lazar's shoes: each day, walking into a high-security facility and coming face to face with technology that, if truly extraterrestrial, would be light-years ahead of human understanding. It's the kind of story that seems straight out of a sci-fi novel. And yet, Bob Lazar spoke about it with such conviction, detailing aspects of the crafts, the workspace, and even the strict security measures.

At the heart of his narrative was Element 115, also known as Moscovium. It's a superheavy element on the periodic table that Lazar asserted was the fuel source for the spacecraft's anti-gravity systems. He described it as a stable isotope, yet unknown and unrecorded by mainstream science at the time. According to Lazar, this element had the extraordinary ability to produce a gravitational field when bombarded with protons, thereby allowing the craft to bend space and effectively "fall" toward its destination at incredible speeds, seemingly breaking the cosmic speed limit set by the light.

Lazar's detailed descriptions of the craft's inner workings painted a picture of alien engineering, with components that were seamlessly integrated in ways that human technology could not replicate. He talked of a reactor that sat like a ball in the center of the craft, omni-directional seats that hinted at the vessels' ability to maneuver in any direction, and the eerie glow that emanated from the propulsion system — all elements that captured the imagination of ufologists and casual observers alike.

Lazar's claims quickly spread like wildfire. Radio shows, TV programs, and newspapers worldwide buzzed with his revelations. Area 51, once just another dot on the Nevada map, became synonymous with UFOs and government secrets. Yet, as fascinating as his story was, it wasn't without its skeptics. Many questioned the authenticity of his claims, pointing to inconsistencies in his narrative or the lack of concrete evidence. Others, however, believed him wholeheartedly, seeing in his testimony a brave attempt to unveil hidden truths.

While detractors pointed to holes in his story, there were parts of Lazar's tale that seemed eerily true. One of the most intriguing was his mention of Element 115. At the time, this element wasn't recognized in scientific circles. But years later, scientists did indeed add Element 115, Moscovium, to the periodic table.

Another point of contention was Lazar's educational background. He claimed to have studied at both MIT and Caltech, yet no records of his attendance at these institutions could be found. Skeptics viewed this as a glaring red flag, suggesting that Lazar might have fabricated parts, if not all, of his story. But Lazar's supporters argue that his background might have been erased or concealed as part of a broader government cover-up.

Amid the swirling whirlpool of belief and skepticism, Lazar tried to return to a semblance of normalcy. He moved away from the media's glare, starting a business dealing with scientific equipment. Yet, the shadow of his claims about Area 51 continued to loom large. Documentaries were made, books written, and even today, the debate about the veracity of his story rages on.

In the end, Bob Lazar's legacy is as enigmatic as the man himself. Was he truly a whistleblower, trying to shed light on one of the government's most tightly guarded secrets? Or was he a master storyteller, spinning a tale that captivated the world's imagination? Whatever the truth, his story has cemented its place in the annals of UFO lore, reminding us all of the ever-present human desire to look up at the stars and wonder.

JOSEPH McMONEAGLE

Can Joseph McMoneagle really see places, people, and events far away or in the future through his mind alone?

How did McMoneagle's alleged psychic abilities help the U.S. government's secretive operations?

In the shadowy world of espionage and secret missions, one name stands out for having a skill straight out of a comic book—Joseph McMoneagle. Picture a man who could, supposedly, close his eyes and see what was happening across the world or even predict events before they happened. Sounds like a superhero, right? But for McMoneagle, this was no fantasy; it was his reality—or so many believed.

Growing up in Miami, Florida in the 1950s, Joseph was an ordinary boy with an ordinary life. But everything changed one day when he had a near-death experience. As doctors fought to save him, Joseph experienced something profound and inexplicable. He recalls floating above his own body, watching the desperate attempts to bring him back to life, and feeling an overwhelming sense of peace. He saw a tunnel, felt a pull towards a light that promised answers to all the mysteries of life, and heard voices whispering truths he couldn't quite grasp.

This near-death experience, commonly known as an NDE, was the catalyst for Joseph's lifelong interest in psychic phenomena. When he miraculously recovered, he couldn't shake the sense that the border between this world and the next was thinner than he'd ever imagined. He began to read about psychic abilities, devouring books and stories about people who claimed to see beyond the physical world, wondering if his NDE had unlocked something within him.

Fast forward a few years, and McMoneagle was no longer just a kid from Florida; he was a soldier in the

U.S. Army. He served his country with dedication, but what many didn't know was that he had a secret. Joseph claimed to have "remote viewing" abilities—a form of psychic skill that allowed him to visualize distant locations as if he were there.

His story gets even more interesting when the U.S. government got wind of his abilities. Joseph was recruited into a top-secret program called the Stargate Project. This wasn't about space travel or battling aliens; it was about using psychic spies for intelligence gathering. The government wanted to see if people like Joseph could actually "see" into the Soviet Union's bases or predict where conflicts might arise.

One of the most fascinating tales of McMoneagle's career was the time he was tasked with 'seeing' into the past—way into the past. The year was 1984, and Joseph was given a sealed envelope. Inside was a mission, but not just any mission. He was asked to focus his mind on coordinates given to him, which he later found out were for the planet Mars, but not as we know it today—for Mars one million years in the past!

Joseph closed his eyes and described, in detail, what he "saw." He spoke of massive pyramids, an ailing civilization, and tall, thin beings who desperately needed to escape a dire situation. Now, whether you believe in psychics or not, you've got to admit, it's a story that grabs you. Was McMoneagle tapping into a long-lost Martian history, or was it all just a figment of his imagination?

As we pause Joseph McMoneagle's story here, think about the possibilities if his claims were true. What if human minds could indeed reach across time and space? What if our thoughts could reveal secrets hidden from our eyes? Stay tuned, because McMoneagle's journey only gets more mysterious from here.

Now, let's dive into another episode that's just as mind-bending. This time, the year was 1979, and the Cold War was in full swing. Tensions were high, and intelligence was the name of the game. Joseph was given another set of coordinates, but these were closer to home—somewhere in the vast expanse of the Earth's oceans.

With the same quiet focus he'd used to peer into the past, McMoneagle set his sights on the present. What he described next left the room silent: a new class of Soviet submarine, unlike anything known to the U.S. at the time. He detailed its structure, its unique propeller, and even the shape of its missile tubes. Skepticism hung heavy in the air—until, months later, satellite images confirmed the existence of the submarine exactly as Joseph had described. Had McMoneagle's vision genuinely revealed a state secret, or was it a lucky guess amplified by coincidence?

Joseph McMoneagle's talents—whether you chalk them up to psychic ability, intuition, or something else entirely—didn't go unrecognized. He was awarded the Legion of Merit, one of the highest peacetime military awards, for providing intelligence otherwise unattainable. This kind of official acknowledgment had many people wondering just how much the government knew about his abilities and what they were using them for.

When the Stargate Project was eventually declassified and shuttered, Joseph didn't just fade into the background. He wrote books detailing his experiences and participated in scientific studies on remote viewing. He appeared on television, demonstrating his abilities under controlled conditions, and maintained his stance that remote viewing was a real, although misunderstood, phenomenon.

To this day, McMoneagle remains a controversial figure. His claims have both passionate believers and staunch skeptics. Some argue that his visions are too vague and easily molded to fit after-the-fact events, while others point to the government's interest and his military decorations as evidence of his abilities.

As we close the chapter on Joseph McMoneagle, we're left with more questions than answers. Can the mind really see beyond the here and now? Or is the power of suggestion stronger than we realize? What we do know is that Joseph's story invites us to open our minds to the possibilities of human potential, pushing the boundaries of what we believe to be possible.

Part Four

Unexplained Abilities
Survivors
Tricksters
Disappearances

The Wild Child of Aveyron

How did a young boy survive alone in the wild
for years without human contact?

What are the true limits of human nature
when separated from civilization?

In the thick forests of Southern France, where ancient trees stood tall and shadows whispered secrets, a mystery unfolded in the late 18th century. From the depth of these woods emerged a figure unlike any other: a boy, seemingly wild, with matted hair, dirt-covered skin, and a gaze that seemed to belong to both man and beast.

The villagers of Lacaune, a small hamlet nestled among the hills, were the first to witness him. On a chilly day in 1800, the boy suddenly appeared, staggering on the outskirts, his ragged appearance drawing stares and gasps. He seemed to be around 12 years old, but he didn't speak or respond to human interaction. Instead, he grunted and made animal-like noises, moving with a strange agility.

Rumors spread like wildfire. Who was this boy? Some whispered that he was a ghost, a spirit of the forest come to deliver a message. Others believed he might be the last of a hidden tribe, living deep in the forest away from human civilization. And some even murmured about dark tales of children stolen away by forest spirits, only to be returned years later, transformed and barely recognizable.

But amid the tales and speculations, one fact was clear: the boy, now named Victor, had lived in the wild, away from human contact, for several years. How he survived the harsh winters, the predatory animals, and the challenges of the wild remained a profound mystery. It wasn't long before the tale of the 'Wild Boy of Aveyron' reached Paris. Intrigued by the story, Dr. Jean

Marc Gaspard Itard, a young physician, took Victor under his wing. Dr. Itard believed that by studying and educating Victor, he could answer some of the age-old questions about the nature of man and the boundaries between the wild and the civilized.

Victor's life in Paris was a stark contrast to his forest days. Dr. Itard tried various methods to teach him language, social skills, and basic etiquette. Some days showed promise, with Victor exhibiting signs of understanding and learning. But on others, his wild nature would take over, reminding everyone of the dense woods and the mysteries they held.

The more Dr. Itard worked with Victor, the more he wondered. Here was a boy, caught between two worlds - the raw wilderness, and the structured society of humans. The question remained: Could Victor ever truly belong to the world of men? Or was he a spirit of the forest, forever calling him back to the wild?

As days turned into nights and seasons changed, glimpses of Victor's humanity began to shine through. He formed a bond with Madame Guérin, the housekeeper, displaying a level of attachment and trust. They communicated through simple gestures, and although words still eluded him, his eyes spoke volumes. There were times when he would sit by the window, seemingly lost in thought, watching the birds fly by. Perhaps he was reminiscing about his days in the forest, or maybe he was trying to find his place in this new world.

Stories of Victor's progress and challenges reached every corner of Paris. Many came to see the "wild boy," some out of sheer curiosity, while others wished to learn from him. Among them was a young girl named Marie, who began visiting Victor. Their bond grew strong, and in her presence, Victor seemed more at ease, laughing and playing like any other teenager.

Yet, the shadows of his past lingered. There were nights when Victor would be gripped by nightmares, and at times, the wild boy of Aveyron would resurface, reminding everyone of the mysteries of nature.

As years passed, Dr. Itard faced a difficult truth. While Victor had made remarkable progress, he would never be fully integrated into society as a typical individual. But that wasn't necessarily a tragic ending. Victor's life was a story of the human spirit and the profound impact of love, patience, and understanding.

In the volumes of history, the story of Victor of Aveyron stands out not just as a tale of a boy lost and found, but as a reflection of humanity's quest to understand itself. Victor's journey from the dense woods of Aveyron to the heart of Paris forces us to ask: What truly makes us human?

In the end, Victor's life remains a mystery. Through him, we're reminded of the thin line that separates the civilized from the wild and the power of hope, love, and the human spirit.

St. Joseph of Cupertino

Could St. Joseph of Cupertino actually float in the air?

Or is there more to the story behind his supposed ability to levitate?

N ow, let's buckle up and zoom back to the 17th century, to a little town in Italy called Cupertino. Here, we meet Joseph, a kid whose head was always in the clouds, literally and figuratively. He wasn't what you'd call a whiz kid. In fact, school was a struggle for him; his report cards were a mix of bad grades and teacher comments like "Needs to pay more attention" and "Daydreams too much."

But Joseph was special in a way that no one could have guessed. He wasn't just the kid who couldn't focus on his homework; he had moments that left those around him absolutely stunned.

Our first tale takes us to a quiet room in a monastery. Picture this: a young Joseph, now a Franciscan monk, deep in prayer. The room is silent, the air still. Suddenly, something astonishing happens. Joseph begins to rise from the floor, his body lifting into the air as if he's as light as a feather. He hovers there, in a serene trance, with a peaceful smile as the other monks rush in, their jaws dropping. They can't believe their eyes. This isn't something you see every day, after all.

This wasn't a one-time event. Joseph became quite famous for these "flights," which seemed to happen whenever he was deep in prayer or when he felt overwhelmed by the beauty of a religious service. It was said that he levitated in front of crowds so often that he was invited to demonstrate his gift to the Pope himself!

The second story is even more mind-blowing. During a religious procession on the feast day of St. Francis of Assisi, something miraculous occurred. As the crowd sang and prayed, moving through the streets with the rhythm of a serene and solemn dance, Joseph was suddenly uplifted, not just in spirit but in body. He soared over the crowd, gliding past wide-eyed townsfolk, up and over the procession, and landed gently in front of a statue of the Virgin Mary. To the people of Cupertino, it was a clear sign of divine favor. To others, it was a mystery wrapped in a riddle.

These stories of Joseph's "flights" spread like wildfire, and soon, people from all over were talking about the flying friar. Some were skeptical, of course. They thought there had to be a trick or an explanation. But those who had witnessed Joseph's flights were convinced they had seen a miracle.

Despite the awe-inspiring stories that surrounded him, Joseph's life wasn't all smooth flying. The Church, cautious of trickery and false miracles, decided to investigate. Joseph was observed, questioned, and tested. Some folks wanted to dismiss his flights as mere tricks or illusions, but no evidence of deception was ever found. In fact, Joseph's simplicity and genuine nature often left his doubters scratching their heads in bewilderment.

But let's zoom in on one particular investigation that put Joseph's life under a microscope. It happened in a quiet, secluded monastery where he was sent away from the public eye. The Church officials had heard enough rumors and wanted to see for themselves what was really going on. For months, Joseph lived under the watchful eyes of the Church, his every move scrutinized. And during this time, something remarkable happened—or, more accurately, didn't happen. Joseph didn't levitate. Not even once.

The investigators were puzzled. Was it stage fright? Was the holy man faking it all along and now couldn't perform under pressure? But then, during a particularly moving church service, it happened. Joseph, caught up in the fervor of the moment, lifted off the ground in front of everyone. It was the undeniable moment the investigators had been waiting for, and it left them stunned. There was no denying what they had seen with their own eyes.

Joseph's story reminds us that the world is full of mysteries, and sometimes, no amount of logic or investigation can explain them away. He lived out his days in that monastery, occasionally surprising his fellow monks with a spontaneous levitation. And as word of his "flights" continued to spread, he became a symbol of hope and wonder, a saint who literally rose above the challenges of his life.

Whether Joseph's flights were miracles, the workings of the mind, or something else entirely, they remind us to keep our minds open and our spirits ready to soar.

For teens reading this, remember that the world is full of extraordinary stories. Who knows? Perhaps one day, you might find yourself adding your own chapter to the endless book of history's mysteries.

GIL PEREZ

Did Gil Pérez truly teleport thousands of miles in an instant?

If not, how did a Spanish guard from the Philippines end up in Mexico City overnight?of his imagination?

Imagine this: You're standing guard, eyes forward, protecting a grand palace. The sun is hot, the armor is heavy, and you're probably daydreaming about lunch. Then, in the blink of an eye, the surroundings change. The buildings look different, the air feels cooler, and the people are speaking a slightly different dialect. You've just traveled over 9,000 miles without taking a single step. Sounds like a wild fantasy, right? But for Gil Pérez, this bizarre tale might have been a reality.

In the late 1500s, the world was a vast and mysterious place. The Spanish Empire spanned across continents, with colonies stretching from Europe to the Americas and onto the islands of Asia. Communication between these places took months, if not years. Yet, if legends are to be believed, one man made that journey in mere moments.

Gil Pérez was a Spanish soldier stationed in Manila, the capital of the Philippines. His duty? To guard the Palacio del Gobernador, the residence of the colonial governor. On a particular day in 1593, something extraordinary happened. After hearing the tragic news of the assassination of Governor Gómez Pérez Dasmariñas, a tired Pérez leaned against a wall and closed his eyes for just a moment.

But when he opened them, the world around him had transformed. Gone were the familiar streets of Manila, replaced by the bustling squares of Mexico City. Confused and dazed, Pérez continued to do what he knew best: he stood guard. The problem? He was wearing the uniform of the guards in the Philippines, not the ones in Mexico. And when asked, Pérez had no idea how he had ended up thousands of miles away from his post.

News of this mysterious soldier spread rapidly. How did he arrive in Mexico City? Some said it was witchcraft, others believed it was a miracle, and a few thought Pérez was simply lying. But one fact puzzled everyone: Pérez was aware of the assassination of the governor in Manila — a piece of news that hadn't yet reached Mexico.

While local authorities tried to figure out the mystery, Pérez was put in jail. They just couldn't believe his story. But, after a couple of months, a ship from the Philippines arrived with news. They confirmed the assassination of the governor and, to everyone's astonishment, recognized Pérez. They vouched for his position as a guard in Manila and were equally baffled about his sudden appearance in Mexico.

As the days turned into weeks, the buzz around Pérez's inexplicable journey began to fade. There were no answers, only speculations. Some said he was abducted by aliens, while others believed he stepped into a mysterious portal. Some even thought he might have discovered a wrinkle in time and space, long before scientists even considered such possibilities.

Whatever the explanation, the legend of Gil Pérez reminds us that history is not just about dates and battles; it's also about mysteries that challenge our understanding of the world. And as you dive into this tale, remember to keep an open mind, for in history, sometimes fact can be stranger than fiction.

While in jail, Pérez's demeanor was unshakably calm. He recounted his tale consistently without a hint of exaggeration, further deepening the mystery. And in a world where tales of sea monsters, dragons, and other fantastical events were part of the everyday conversation, the idea of instantaneous travel, though bizarre, found some degree of acceptance.

Amid all the debate and speculation, two Dominican priests took a keen interest in Pérez's tale. They visited him in jail, interviewing him at length. Intriguingly, they later noted that Pérez showed genuine signs of disorientation and culture shock. He was unfamiliar with certain customs of Mexico, despite being a Spanish soldier, and was adamant about returning to his post in Manila.

The priests, after cross-referencing Pérez's claims with incoming sailors and other witnesses, began to believe that his story might just be genuine. They petitioned for his release and eventually, Pérez was set free. He was not returned to Manila immediately but was kept under observation in Mexico City. Records then show that he did, after a while, board a ship that was making its way back to the Philippines.

Upon his return to Manila, Pérez was greeted with mixed reactions. While some saw him as a curiosity or even a celebrity, others remained skeptical of his claims. To many, he was simply the soldier who had deserted his post, regardless of the extraordinary circumstances he described.

Life for Pérez after the event is largely undocumented. Did he continue his service in Manila? Did he ever experience another such mysterious event? The answers remain elusive.

The tale of Gil Pérez is more than just an account of a mysterious journey. It's a testament to the human fascination with the unexplained. It reminds us that even in an age of exploration and discovery, there are things that remain beyond our understanding.

TARRARE

How was Tarrare able to consume such
massive amounts of food and odd objects
without suffering severe health consequences?

What might have caused his insatiable
appetite?

In the bustling streets of 18th-century France, amidst the grandeur of palaces and the chatter of marketplaces, a peculiar figure emerged, casting a long, mysterious shadow. His name? Tarrare. Not a king, not a warrior, but a man with an appetite so bizarre that it would be remembered for centuries to come.

Born in rural France around 1772, Tarrare's early life was, to put it mildly, unusual. By the age of 17, he could consume a quarter of a cow's weight in beef in a single day! To put that into perspective, imagine eating about 100 large cheeseburgers... for breakfast. And his diet wasn't limited to food either. He was known to munch on corks, stones, and even live animals.

One might wonder, "Did he look different because of his unique eating habits?" Well, surprisingly, Tarrare was of average height and didn't appear overweight. However, when he hadn't eaten, his skin would sag, especially around his stomach, giving him an almost deflated look.

His extraordinary appetite caught the attention of many, including the military. "Aha!" they thought. "Perhaps we can use his unusual skills for our advantage." And so, Tarrare was employed by the French army as a sort of human courier. They believed he could safely "transport" documents by swallowing them. His most famous mission involved him swallowing a wooden box containing secret documents. However, this endeavor didn't go as planned. He got caught, became ill, and the mission was deemed a failure.

Even the world of medicine couldn't resist the allure of Tarrare's mysteries. Dr. Percy, a top physician of the time, took Tarrare under his observation. Despite the vast quantities Tarrare consumed, he seemed malnourished and was constantly hungry. Dr. Percy tried, unsuccessfully, to curb his appetite with various treatments.

Tarrare's life was filled with curiosity, fear, and astonishment from those around him. From attempting to drink the blood of patients in a hospital to suspiciously lingering around a pharmacy, he never ceased to shock those who encountered him.

While many saw Tarrare as a medical marvel or a tool to be used, his life wasn't easy. He was an outcast, often treated more as an experiment than a human. Despite the attention, fame, and intrigue, Tarrare's story is as much about the mysteries of the human body as it is about the loneliness of being different.

The questions surrounding Tarrare's condition multiplied with every passing day. Was he cursed? Was he blessed? As tales of his incredible feats spread far and wide, Tarrare became something of a legend in his own time. But behind the gasps of astonishment lay a tragic story of a man in search of understanding and acceptance.

Dr. Percy, despite his initial curiosity and genuine attempts to help, struggled to find a solution to Tarrare's condition. From laudanum to tobacco pills, from sour wine to soft-boiled eggs, the good doctor tried every remedy he knew, but Tarrare's appetite remained as

132

ravenous as ever. What was even more puzzling was that Tarrare did not gain weight, no matter how much he consumed.

After Tarrare's stay under Dr. Percy's care, details about Tarrare's life became murkier. Rumors whispered that he took to the streets, performing acts of bizarre eating for money. His appearance grew gaunt, his eyes more haunted, as if the weight of his own mysteries was bearing down on him.

Several years later, Tarrare's story found a sorrowful ending. He turned up at a hospital in Versailles, weakened and weary. The doctors, upon examining him, found that he was suffering from advanced tuberculosis. A short while later, Tarrare passed away, leaving behind a legacy filled with more questions than answers.

To this day, Tarrare's condition remains a medical enigma. Some believe he had a damaged amygdala, the part of the brain responsible for regulating hunger. Others speculate about rare metabolic conditions. But the truth remains veiled in mystery.

In the annals of history, Tarrare stands as a testament to the incredible complexities of the human body and spirit. His story reminds us that sometimes, the lines between marvel and malady are blurred. It asks us to be compassionate to those who are different and to always seek understanding, even when faced with the incomprehensible. For in the end, Tarrare wasn't just a man with an endless hunger; he was a soul in search of belonging.

ᕰHINEᴀS GᴀGE

How did Phineas Gage survive such a
catastrophic injury to the brain?

Why did Gage's personality undergo such a
dramatic transformation after the accident, and
what does it reveal about the workings of the
human brain?

In the small town of Cavendish, Vermont, in 1848, the rhythmic clinking of hammers against iron echoed through the air. Railroad construction was in full swing, with workers busily laying down tracks that would connect the town to the rest of the world. Among these hardworking folks was 25-year-old Phineas Gage, known to be one of the most responsible and efficient foremen on the job.

On the 13th of September, a day that started just like any other, Phineas was packing explosive powder into a hole to blast away rocks, making space for the railroad tracks. He used a tamping iron, a long, rod-like tool, to pack the powder down. But in a fateful moment, there was a spark, followed by an explosion.

The tamping iron, which was over three feet long and weighed 13 pounds, shot upwards, piercing through Phineas's cheek, passing behind his left eye, and exiting through the top of his head. The rod landed several yards away, smeared with blood and brain matter. The scene was gruesome, and anyone would have assumed that Phineas was done for.

But here's where the story takes a turn for the unbelievable: Phineas didn't die. In fact, he didn't even lose consciousness! Moments after the accident, he sat up, speaking and walking with only minor assistance. He was taken to a nearby inn, where Dr. John Harlow, the local physician, took over his care.

News of the accident spread like wildfire. It wasn't just the miraculous survival that had people talking; it was also Gage's bizarre behavior in the days and weeks that followed. The once-respectable and mild-mannered foreman began to change.

The townspeople were in for a shock. Gage's language became filled with cuss words and profanities, something quite scandalous in the 19th century, especially from a man who had previously been so polite. He grew restless and impatient, often making hasty decisions without any regard for consequences. The Phineas Gage that Cavendish once knew seemed to have vanished, replaced by someone entirely different.

Dr. Harlow, who had been documenting the case closely, noted these personality shifts with great interest. He wrote in his medical reports how Phineas was "fitful, irreverent, indulging at times in the grossest profanity". The transformation was so drastic that Phineas's employers felt he was no longer fit for his role as a foreman.

This was a time when neuroscience was in its infancy. The brain was still a largely uncharted territory, and Gage's case became a focal point for debates among scientists and doctors. They pondered over how a rod piercing through certain parts of the brain could lead to such dramatic personality changes.

As months turned into years, Phineas tried to reintegrate into society. He took on various jobs, including a stint in a stable in New Hampshire and as a stagecoach driver in way down in Chile. The role in Chile was particularly fitting since it required quick reflexes and decision-making skills—traits that the new Phineas had in abundance.

However, Gage's health started to deteriorate. He began having seizures and, in 1860, just twelve years after the accident, Phineas Gage passed away. But the legend of Phineas Gage lived on, far outlasting the man himself.

Today, Phineas Gage is a cornerstone in the study of neuroscience and psychology. His case offers a window into how different parts of the brain contribute to our personality and behavior. It's taught in classrooms around the world as an example of how injuries to the brain can affect personality.

In the end, Phineas Gage's story serves as a testament to the resilience of the human spirit and the mysteries of the human brain. While many saw him as a medical oddity, others viewed him as a man who faced unimaginable adversity and tried to carve out a life in a world that could no longer understand him. The tamping iron that once shot through his brain is now on display at the Warren Anatomical Museum in Boston, serving as a tangible reminder of the man and the mystery that was Phineas Gage.

Bobby Dunbar

Who was the boy that the Dunbars claimed to be their missing son?

What truly happened to Bobby Dunbar on that fateful day at the lake?

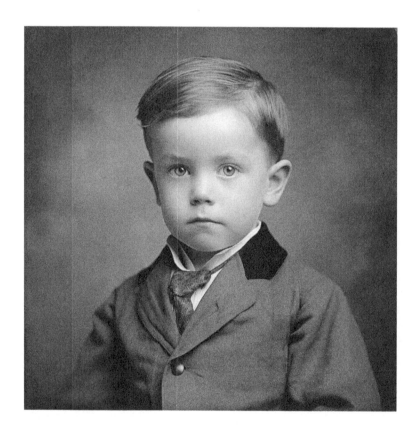

The summer sun cast its radiant glow over the picturesque Swayze Lake in Louisiana. Families gathered for picnics, children's laughter echoed, and the sweet scent of blooming wildflowers permeated the air. It was August 1912, a time when summer adventures were born. But for the Dunbar family, this trip would be remembered for a very different reason.

Bobby Dunbar was an energetic four-year-old with curly blond hair and a mischievous twinkle in his eye. On that sunny day, he and his family, including his parents Lessie and Percy Dunbar, decided to spend the day by the lake. Bobby, with the endless curiosity of a child, wandered off to explore. Hours went by, and when the sun began its descent, casting long shadows on the ground, a horrifying realization dawned on the Dunbars: Bobby was nowhere to be found.

The atmosphere at the lake quickly shifted from one of joy to panic. Whispers turned into shouts, casual strolls turned into frantic searches. The local community rallied, combing every inch of the area, dredging the lake, and even looking for alligator dens, fearing the worst. Days turned into weeks, and despite their relentless search, there was no sign of young Bobby. The heartbroken Dunbars returned home, clinging to the fragile hope that someday, somehow, their boy might return.

Almost eight months passed with no news, and then, a breakthrough. In Mississippi, a wandering handyman named William Cantwell Walters was arrested. With him was a boy fitting Bobby's description. Walters insisted the boy was Charles Bruce Anderson, the son of a woman who worked for his family. But the Dunbars were convinced: the boy, they believed, was their missing Bobby.

Reunited with his alleged family, the boy was quickly reintegrated into the Dunbar household. But here's where the story takes a perplexing turn. While the Dunbars were certain they had their son back, others, including some family members, were not so sure. The boy seemed different, quieter, and less spirited than the Bobby they remembered.

Julia Anderson, the mother of Charles Bruce, arrived to claim her son. Heartbreakingly, the boy did not immediately recognize her, and with no concrete evidence to support her claim, she returned home, childless.

For the Dunbars, the return of "Bobby" was bittersweet. While they had their son back, whispers of doubt echoed throughout the community. The media latched onto the story, adding layers of speculation, intrigue, and drama. Some believed the Dunbars, while others were convinced the boy was indeed Charles Bruce Anderson.

In the midst of this emotional whirlwind, two families were torn apart, and one child stood at the center of a mystery that baffled a nation. The truth seemed as elusive as a summer breeze, and as the years rolled by, the question remained: who was the boy the Dunbars called Bobby?

The ensuing legal battle was both publicized and polarizing. Courtrooms overflowed with spectators eager to witness the resolution of this baffling saga. Lawyers for both sides presented their arguments passionately. The Dunbars held fast to their conviction, presenting old photographs, scars, and other marks they believed to prove the boy's identity. On the other side, Julia Anderson's lawyers put forth witnesses who testified to the boy's life before his sudden disappearance with Walters.

As days turned into weeks, the court case began to take a toll on everyone involved. The young boy, whether Bobby or Charles, was shuffled between families, his identity constantly under scrutiny. He was questioned, prodded, and examined by numerous individuals, all of whom hoped to shed some light on his true lineage.

After a grueling trial, the court finally gave its verdict: the boy was declared to be Bobby Dunbar. Julia Anderson left the courthouse in tears, her heart shattered. She went back home, maintaining until her last breath that the Dunbars had her son. Life for the Dunbars, however, was forever changed. They tried to move forward, to provide a normal life for Bobby. Yet, whispers never ceased. Their neighbors, friends, and even strangers continued to speculate and theorize about the boy's real identity.

The Dunbar case slowly faded from national news, replaced by other events and stories. But within the family, the scars remained. Bobby grew up under the Dunbar name, eventually getting married and having children of his own. He rarely spoke about the ordeal, and the memories of those tumultuous years were mostly locked away.

It wasn't until nearly a century later, with the advancement of DNA technology, that the mystery saw a potential resolution. In 2004, some of Bobby's descendants decided to put the rumors and speculations to rest. They underwent DNA testing, comparing their genetic markers to those of the Dunbar lineage. The results were startling: the DNA did not match. This confirmed that the boy who had lived as Bobby Dunbar was, in fact, not a blood relative of the Dunbar family.

The revelation sent shockwaves through the descendants of both the Dunbar and Anderson families. For some, it was a vindication of long-held beliefs. For others, it was a heartbreaking realization that a family member had lived his entire life under a mistaken identity.

Today, the story of Bobby Dunbar serves as a haunting reminder of the complexities of human nature, memory, and the lengths to which families will go to reunite with lost loved ones. The boy's true identity, whether Bobby or Charles or someone else entirely, remains one of history's most intriguing puzzles.

PRAHLAD JANI

Could a person truly live without consuming
food or water for decades?

What secrets of human endurance and
spirituality might be hidden within Jani's unique
tale?

In the rich variety of India's stories, where myth and reality weave together, there emerges the tale of Prahlad Jani, a man who claimed to have spent more than seven decades without food or water. For most of us, skipping lunch is an ordeal, but imagine abstaining from all food for years on end!

Born in 1929, Prahlad Jani's story begins in a small village in the Indian state of Gujarat. As a child, Jani felt a calling that was different from others. At the tender age of seven, he left home, venturing into the lush jungles of Gujarat. Here, amidst the whispering trees and serene temples, Jani would come across a band of wandering holy men, or sadhus.

The sadhus lived a life of austerity, denying themselves earthly pleasures in pursuit of spiritual enlightenment. Under their guidance, young Jani began to meditate and engage in spiritual practices. But what set him apart was a unique claim: the goddess Amba, he said, had bestowed upon him a special gift. He no longer needed food or water to survive. The energy of the universe, or "prana" as it's known in Hindu philosophy, sustained him.

Word of Jani's unusual lifestyle spread like wildfire. How could someone, especially a youngster, survive without the basic sustenance? Many dismissed it as a tall tale, a story cooked up to draw attention. But Jani remained steadfast in his claims.

In the 1970s, curiosity around Jani peaked when local newspapers began reporting about the "breatharian monk" who had supposedly not eaten or drunk anything for decades. His story caught the attention of not just the common people but also of scientists and researchers.

They wondered: Could Jani's claims have a grain of truth? Was it possible for the human body to sustain itself without food or water for such extended periods? Determined to find out, a team of doctors decided to observe Jani closely. Under strict surveillance, Jani was placed in a hospital, watched around the clock by doctors and cameras to ensure he didn't secretly consume anything. The initial skepticism of the doctors was understandable. After all, humans typically can't survive more than a week without water!

Days turned into weeks, and to the astonishment of the medical team, Jani displayed no signs of hunger or dehydration. He seemed perfectly healthy, going about his daily routines of meditation and prayer, all while remaining disconnected from the basic human need to eat and drink. The results of the observation left the medical community baffled. How was Jani defying the known limits of human biology? Scientists scrambled to figure out if Jani's body had somehow adapted to extract energy from other sources or if there was another explanation entirely.

However, not everyone was convinced. Some critics pointed out potential flaws in the experiments, while others wondered if there was more to Jani's story than met the eye. As the news of Jani's mysterious abilities spread far and wide, he became something of a legend in India. Pilgrims and curious onlookers began traveling from all corners of the country to meet the man who claimed to live without sustenance. Some came seeking blessings, some in search of spiritual guidance, and others purely out of curiosity.

Jani's humble home turned into a space of solace for many. Here was a man, untouched by the needs and desires that consumed most humans. Instead of basking in the limelight, Jani continued his spiritual practices, meditating for long hours, and occasionally sharing his insights with those who sought him out.

But Jani's life wasn't without controversy. Skeptics continually challenged his claims. They argued that the human body, as we understand it, simply cannot function without food and water. They believed that there had to be some trick or secret that Jani was keeping. There were accusations of hidden food sources and secret water stashes. But no concrete evidence ever emerged to debunk Jani's claims.

In 2010, Jani once again volunteered for scientific observation. This time, a team of 30 specialists monitored him. For 15 days, he was kept under a strict watch in a hospital. And once again, the results were the same: Jani showed no signs of hunger or thirst, did not eat or drink, and yet remained perfectly healthy.

Scientists were stumped. Theories abounded — from Jani having a unique metabolism to him harnessing some form of unknown energy. Some suggested that Jani was a living testament to the power of meditation and yoga, ancient Indian practices that are known to control and transform the body's energies.

As the years passed, Jani aged but his story remained timeless. Whether he was a medical mystery, a spiritual wonder, or something else entirely, remained a topic of debate.

At age 91, Prahlad Jani passed away in 2020, but the enigma surrounding his life lingers on. How could a man defy the very basics of human biology? Was it sheer willpower, divine intervention, or an unsolved scientific phenomenon?

As the chapter of Prahlad Jani's life comes to a close, it leaves us with profound questions about the human body, spirituality, and the thin boundary between belief and reality. Jani's story challenges our understanding of the possible and asks us to ponder: how much do we truly know about the mysteries of existence?

Wolf Messing

Could Wolf Messing truly read minds, or was
he the master of understanding human
behavior?

How did Messing allegedly predict significant
historical events with such accuracy?

In the shadows of history, there are tales that teeter on the edge of reality and myth, stories that make us question the very limits of human capability. One such story is that of Wolf Messing, a man whose mind seemed to hold the keys to secrets untold. Born in 1899 in Poland, Messing's life read like a page out of a mystical thriller, filled with mind-reading, predictions, and escapes that baffled all who witnessed them.

One of the most gripping tales of Messing's mysterious abilities unfolded in the heart of Warsaw. It was the 1920s, and Messing, a young man with sharp eyes and a knowing smile, claimed he could read minds. Skeptics snorted at the idea, and one day, a group of them challenged him to prove his powers. They told him to perform a bank heist, but not the kind you're picturing. There would be no masks or secret notes; instead, Messing was to use his alleged telepathic abilities to rob a bank without a whisper of threat or violence.

The next day, Messing walked calmly into one of Warsaw's busiest banks. He handed the teller a deposit slip. The teller, under what seemed to be the spell of Messing's intense gaze, handed over the equivalent of 100,000 zlotys without question. Messing walked out as calmly as he had entered, with a bag of money in hand. But here's the jaw-dropping twist: the deposit slip wasn't a request for cash at all. It was a blank piece of paper.

Word of this mind-boggling heist spread like wildfire. The police caught up with Messing, but upon investigating, they were left scratching their heads in disbelief. The tellers were adamant they'd seen a legitimate transaction request. It was as if Messing had cast a spell, changing what they saw with the sheer force of his will. No charges were pressed; after all, how do you prosecute someone for using mind control?

Another tale that cements Messing's legacy occurred during his encounter with one of history's most fearsome leaders: Joseph Stalin. Stalin, intrigued and perhaps seeking to unmask Messing as a fraud, invited him to perform a private demonstration. The task was a mind-bending game of hide and seek, where Messing was to locate the hidden Stalin without a single hint.

Stalin, confident in the secrecy of his hiding spot, waited. Yet, within a short time, Messing walked straight to Stalin's hideout, a place no one could have guessed. When asked how he did it, Messing simply claimed he read Stalin's thoughts, which led him to the spot. Whether it was an uncanny perception or true telepathy, Messing's feat left even Stalin, a man not easily impressed or outwitted, silently astounded.

Among his numerous legendary tales, another incident stands out, not only for its daring but for the high stakes it involved. During World War II, Messing, who was Jewish, found himself in a perilous position as the Nazi regime swept across Europe. He made a bold and chilling prediction that Hitler would meet his downfall if he turned to invade Russia. When this prediction reached the ears of the Nazi high command, a bounty was put on Messing's head, forcing him to employ his elusive skills to survive.

Messing's ability to escape capture was nothing short of miraculous. It's said that he disguised himself and used his skills to mentally persuade German soldiers at checkpoints to let him pass. The soldiers, perhaps under the influence of his compelling presence, saw not a wanted man, but an unremarkable civilian. Messing's journey through the dangers of wartime Europe seemed to be aided by his mysterious gift, allowing him to slip through the cracks of the Nazis time and time again.

After the war, Messing's reputation only grew. He became known not only as a performer but also as someone who could offer insights into the human psyche. In a world trying to rebuild itself, the idea that someone could see into the hearts and minds of others offered both hope and fear. Was there truly a man who could know your deepest thoughts and intentions?

In the classrooms of today, Wolf Messing's name may not be as well-known as other historical figures, but his life story poses questions that are timeless. In an age where your every thought can be Tweeted or Snapchatted, the idea of someone "reading" those thoughts without a digital footprint is both intriguing and unsettling.

Was Wolf Messing a true mentalist with an extraordinary gift, or was he simply the greatest actor of his time, a master of intuition and suggestion? While historians and skeptics may debate the truth, the stories of his remarkable life continue to inspire wonder and curiosity among those who hear them, prompting us all to explore the endless possibilities of the human mind.

TIBETAN TUMMO MONKS

How do the Tummo monks generate intense
body heat in the freezing Himalayan
temperatures, clad only in thin, wet sheets?

Is their ability to control body temperature
using meditation scientifically explainable or is it
a supernatural phenomenon?

The mighty Himalayas! Towering peaks of snow and rock, where the air is thin, and temperatures drop to bone-chilling lows. Yet, amidst this icy world, a group of monks possesses a power that seems almost magical.

Picture this: a frozen lake surrounded by snowy mountains. It's a place where even the bravest might think twice before venturing out without thick jackets, scarves, and gloves. But then, you see them – monks dressed in thin robes, sitting calmly on the icy ground, meditating. What's even more baffling? They're wrapped in wet sheets. In minutes, steam starts rising, and the sheets begin to dry!

This isn't a scene from a fantasy novel; it's a real-life display of the power of Tummo meditation. The Tummo monks, residing in the high-altitude monasteries of Tibet, have mastered an ancient form of meditation that allows them to control their body temperature. The word "Tummo" means "inner fire", and that's precisely what these monks seem to ignite within themselves.

Legend has it that Tummo meditation was developed by Tibetan yogis who sought to find ways to stay warm in the harsh mountain climate. But over time, this technique became much more than just a survival tool— it evolved into a spiritual practice aimed at reaching a deep state of inner peace and enlightenment.

Imagine being 13 and trying to concentrate on your homework with the TV blaring, your siblings squabbling, and your phone buzzing with messages. It's hard, right? Now, imagine trying to concentrate so hard that you can raise your body temperature in the freezing cold. That's the level of focus these monks achieve. Stories of their extraordinary feats have traveled far and wide. Some speak of monks melting snow around them just by sitting on it. Others tell tales of them surviving nights in freezing caves without any source of warmth.

But is there any truth to these tales? Can the human body truly be controlled with such precision through mere thought and concentration? Or are the Tummo monks harnessing a power that goes beyond our understanding?

As more people from around the world started hearing about these almost superhuman monks, scientists grew curious. They began arriving in Tibet with thermal cameras, monitoring devices, and a barrage of questions. Were the Tummo monks ready to share the secrets of their "inner fire"? And if they did, would science be able to explain it?

As we delve deeper into the enigma of Tummo, prepare to be both amazed and puzzled by the tales and truths of the monks who've harnessed the power of fire from within.

As science often does when faced with mysteries, researchers set up experiments to understand the Tummo monks' techniques better. Monks were invited to demonstrate their skills in controlled settings, away from their icy mountain retreats and into modern labs filled with machines and monitors. One particular experiment stood out. A renowned scientist draped wet, cold sheets around a monk in a chilly room. Most people would shiver uncontrollably, their teeth chattering in the cold. But the monk? He sat still, going deep into meditation. Before long, the wet sheets started steaming! And in just a short time, they were dry. The readings from the machines showed that the monk's body temperature had risen significantly. The room, filled with the cold, analytical air of science, was touched by a warmth that went beyond mere temperature.

But how did they do it? Well, the monks explained that Tummo meditation involved a combination of breathing techniques, visualization, and rhythmic chanting. By imagining a flame within their core and syncing their breath with specific chants, they could activate their body's internal heat. But, as one monk gently reminded the scientists, it wasn't just about the physical. The spiritual aspect, the connection to the universe and to the divine, played an equally vital role.

Amidst the experiments, the monks continued their practices undisturbed, their focus unwavering. For them, Tummo wasn't about proving a point or showcasing a skill. It was a spiritual journey, a path to enlightenment, and a connection with the universe.

In the end, while science made strides in understanding the physical aspects of Tummo, the spiritual essence remained elusive. As the sun sets behind the Himalayas and the cold winds sweep across its vast expanse, the Tummo monks sit in meditation, their "inner fires" burning bright, a testament to the incredible power of the human spirit and mind.

Ngoc Thai

**How has Ngoc Thai managed to survive
without sleep for so many years?**

**What can his unique condition teach us about
the science of sleep and its importance to
human health?**

Imagine, just for a moment, the coziest bed you've ever slept in. Soft pillows, warm blankets, the comforting embrace of sleep after a long day... Sounds perfect, doesn't it? Now, what if you couldn't sleep, not just for one night, or two, but for years? It's a baffling idea, but for one man named Ngoc Thai, it was his reality.

In a small village in Vietnam, where the roosters herald the dawn and families gather around fires to share tales of the day, lived Ngoc, a man with an extraordinary story. He was just like any other farmer, tending to his crops and caring for his family, with one exception: he hadn't slept in decades. It all began one fateful night in the late 1970s. After a particularly exhausting day, Ngoc lay down to rest, waiting for sleep to take over. But it didn't. Hours turned into days, days into weeks, and before he knew it, a whole year had passed without a single moment of sleep. While most of us would be zombie-like, struggling to function, Ngoc continued his daily routines seemingly unaffected.

Villagers whispered among themselves, some in awe, others in disbelief. Many nights, curious neighbors would stealthily peer through Ngoc's window, half-expecting to catch him in a secret slumber. But every time, they'd find him wide awake, often reading or working on some household chore.

News of the "sleepless wonder" spread beyond his village. Scientists and doctors from around the world flocked to study this medical marvel. They conducted tests, tracking his brain waves and monitoring his health.

Yet, every report came back with the same puzzling conclusion: Ngoc Thai was in good health and, indeed, showed no signs of sleep.

But here's where things get even stranger. Not only did he not sleep, but he also claimed he never felt tired or experienced the usual side effects of sleep deprivation like hallucinations or weakened immunity. In fact, Ngoc mentioned feeling more energetic and alert than ever before.

The elders in his village whispered of ancient legends, tales of individuals blessed (or perhaps cursed) with unique gifts. Some said Ngoc had been touched by the spirits, while others believed he had tapped into some hidden reservoir of energy within the human body.

Young teens, like you, would often visit him, eyes wide with fascination. They'd bombard him with questions, "Do you ever dream?" "Do you miss sleeping?" "What do you do all night?" Ngoc would smile patiently, answering each query. But even he admitted he didn't truly understand his condition. He missed the feeling of drifting into dreams, the comfort of a bed, and the simple joy of waking up refreshed.

As the years went by, Ngoc's fame grew, but so did the mystery surrounding his condition. Journalists from far and wide arrived, their cameras flashing, eager to document this living enigma. They'd often find him in his garden, hands deep in the earth, planting seeds or harvesting crops. The man who never slept was also the man who never stopped.

Yet, despite all the attention, Ngoc remained humble. He didn't see himself as special or gifted. To him, he was simply a man who had adjusted to a different rhythm of life. However, adjusting didn't mean it was easy. Nights were the hardest. While his family rested, and the village fell silent, Ngoc felt the weight of solitude. He'd often wander into the nearby woods, listening to the nocturnal songs of nature, finding solace in the company of the moon and stars.

Medical experts continued to be baffled. Sleep, after all, is essential for the human body to heal and regenerate. How was it possible for someone to skip this crucial process and still function normally? Some hypothesized that Ngoc's body had found a way to enter a restful state while awake, a sort of meditation that replaced the need for sleep. Others wondered if his genetic makeup held the secret, possibly a mutation that eliminated the need for rest.

Yet, no theory was ever proven. And as the decades rolled on, the intrigue deepened. Stories of Ngoc's kindness also spread. It was said that he used his extra hours to help others. He'd repair broken tools, build shelters, and even watch over the sick, all under the cover of night. Children in the village began to leave notes outside his home, asking for help with their homework or seeking advice on personal problems. Ngoc became a guardian of sorts, a silent protector in the moonlit hours.

However, like all tales shrouded in mystery, skepticism arose. Some claimed it was all an elaborate hoax, a story blown out of proportion. But those who met Ngoc, who saw the sincerity in his eyes and witnessed his relentless energy, couldn't help but believe.

As our journey through the tale of Ngoc Thai draws to a close, we're reminded of the wonders of the human body and spirit. Ngoc's story challenges our understanding of sleep, health, and the boundaries of what's considered "normal."

So, the next time you lay down, pulling the covers tight and drifting into a dream, think of the man in Vietnam, for whom night is just the beginning of another day.

KEVIN RICHARDSON

How did Kevin Richardson develop such an extraordinary bond with wild lions, defying the natural predator-prey relationship?

What drives him to constantly push the boundaries of human-animal interactions, especially with one of the world's deadliest creatures?

I magine, for a moment, strolling through the golden plains of Africa with a lion by your side. Not just any lion, but a massive, majestic creature known for its raw power and predatory prowess. To most of us, this sounds like a scene straight from a fantasy movie, where magic spells bind man and beast. But for Kevin Richardson, this fantastical image is his everyday reality.

Born in 1971, in the vibrant city of Johannesburg, South Africa, Kevin's love for animals was clear early on. As a child, his backyard adventures with pets showed at a deeper connection with the animal kingdom. Little did anyone know that his love for creatures would evolve into a deep relationship with the kings of the jungle.

As Kevin grew older, his path led him to a rehabilitation center, where injured and orphaned animals were given a second chance at life. It was here that he had his first encounter with lion cubs. While many would see them as dangerous wild animals, Kevin saw souls yearning for connection and understanding. He spent hours, days, then weeks with them, immersing himself in their world. With each gentle touch and soft whisper, he broke down the invisible barriers that stood between man and lion.

But this was just the beginning. As the cubs grew, so did Kevin's bond with them. He became a familiar figure among the pride, not as a threat or food, but as a companion. Videos of Kevin playing, napping, and even swimming with fully grown lions left viewers worldwide in awe and disbelief. Was this man truly fearless, or did he possess a secret that allowed him to befriend these mighty beasts?

His methods were unconventional, to say the least. Instead of using dominance or fear to control the lions, Kevin relied on trust, understanding, and love. He believed that by treating these animals with respect and kindness, they would reciprocate in their unique ways. And they did. Time and time again, Kevin was seen in the midst of a lion pride, being groomed, cuddled, and accepted as one of their own.

But not everyone was impressed. Critics argued that Kevin's interactions were dangerous, not just for him, but for the very lions he claimed to love. They believed that by humanizing these wild creatures, he was stripping them of their natural instincts, making them dependent and potentially more aggressive.

Yet, Kevin stood firm in his beliefs. He felt that his work was shedding light on the delicate balance between humans and nature. In a world where lion populations are dwindling, Kevin's unique relationship with them brought attention to their plight. He hoped that by showcasing the gentler side of these magnificent creatures, people would be inspired to protect and preserve them for future generations.

Meanwhile, people from different parts of the world flocked to see the 'Lion Whisperer' in action. They wanted to experience the magic themselves, to touch and feel these majestic creatures. But Kevin, ever the protector, was cautious. The sanctuary wasn't a zoo; it was a haven where lions could be themselves. So, while he did organize tours, he always ensured the welfare of his beloved lions came first.

However, there were moments that tested Kevin's resolve. One such instance was when a lioness, under his care, acted aggressively towards a visitor. Though no harm was done, it served as a stark reminder of the wild nature of these animals. They weren't pets; they were wild creatures with instincts. Kevin often emphasized this point, "Trust is crucial, but one should never forget what they truly are."

As the years rolled by, Kevin expanded his efforts beyond lions. Hyenas, leopards, and even a few mischievous meerkats found their way into his heart and sanctuary. Each species presented its own set of challenges, but Kevin's approach remained the same: patience, love, and respect.

But perhaps the most significant testament to Kevin's work was the birth of cubs within the sanctuary. Witnessing the circle of life, from playful cubs to majestic adults, was a surreal experience. And as these cubs grew, they too displayed an unusual comfort with Kevin, proving that the bonds he formed were not just fleeting moments but lifelong connections.

Kevin's story is not just about the incredible bond between man and animal. It's a tale that highlights the importance of coexistence, understanding, and respect. In a rapidly changing world where habitats are shrinking, and wildlife is under constant threat, stories like Kevin's offer a beacon of hope.

WIM HOF

How can a person withstand freezing
temperatures for such long periods without
getting frostbite or hypothermia?

Can Wim Hof's methods of combining
breathing exercises and cold exposure truly
boost the immune system and improve mental
well-being?

In a world where superheroes exist mostly on comic book pages and movie screens, imagine stumbling across someone who might just have a superpower of his own. This isn't a tale from a galaxy far away, but the real-life story of a man named Wim Hof, better known as "The Iceman."

Picture this: Snow-capped mountains with temperatures so freezing that just being there would send shivers down your spine. While most of us would be bundled up in heavy coats, scarves, and gloves, there's this one guy, Wim, climbing Mount Kilimanjaro... in nothing but a pair of shorts! Crazy, right? But how did he get here?

Wim's life wasn't always about breaking records or undertaking frosty adventures. Growing up in the Netherlands, he was just like any other kid, playing outside, scraping his knees, and dreaming big. But as he grew older, a deep sadness hit him hard - the loss of his wife. Heartbroken and searching for answers, Wim found solace in the icy embrace of nature. One winter's day, on a whim, he decided to dive into a freezing canal. Instead of the biting cold he expected, he felt an overwhelming sense of peace.

This icy dip was just the beginning of Wim's frosty journey. Intrigued by the calm he felt amidst the cold, he began to explore the power of the mind and body, diving deeper into ancient breathing techniques and meditations. He believed that combining these with regular exposure to cold could help people control their body's reactions, enhance their immune system, and even boost their mood.

As the years went by, Wim's experiments with cold became more and more daring. He wasn't just taking cold showers anymore; he was running marathons in icy deserts, hiking up snow-covered peaks, and even standing encased in blocks of ice—all while barely wearing a thing! And, as baffling as it was, he seemed perfectly fine, even thriving in conditions that would have most of us running for a cozy blanket and a cup of hot cocoa.

Word quickly spread about the man who could defy the cold. People from all over the world, scientists, athletes, and even curious teenagers, started wondering: What's the Iceman's secret? Can we all tap into this superpower? As Wim's teachings spread, scientists started becoming really curious. They had heaps of questions. Was there a special gene that made Wim immune to cold? Was it all just a trick of the mind? So, they put him to the test.

In lab coats and glasses, with machines that beeped and blinked, they observed Wim as he performed his breathing exercises and then was exposed to freezing temperatures. Most people would start shivering uncontrollably, but not Wim. His body temperature remained pretty stable, and he was at ease. The scientists were astonished!

The secret, as Wim explained, lay in his unique breathing technique. By taking deep, rhythmic breaths and holding them in, he believed he could influence his body's inner thermostat and immune response. This was a groundbreaking revelation! Suddenly, the mysteries of ancient practices met the wonders of modern science.

But it wasn't just about enduring cold. People who practiced Wim's methods reported feeling happier, less stressed, and more energized. They found they could focus better and even fight off sickness faster. The Iceman's methods weren't just about showing off; they were about living healthier, more vibrant lives.

Of course, there were skeptics and naysayers. Some warned that not everyone should plunge into icy waters or snow hike without proper training. Wim always stressed the importance of learning the techniques safely and never pushing one's limits recklessly. After all, even superheroes need to train.

As the years went on, Wim continued his adventures, setting world records, and inspiring thousands. He swam under ice sheets, ran marathons in the blistering cold, and even attempted to climb Mount Everest in his signature shorts. Every challenge was a testament to human potential, a nudge to explore beyond our boundaries.

Yet, despite all his fame and achievements, Wim remained grounded. To him, the cold was a teacher, nature was a guide, and the mind, an uncharted territory ready to be explored. His message to the world was clear: We all have an 'Iceman' within us. It's just a matter of tapping into that inner strength and discovering our own superpowers.

TIM CRIDLAND

How can Tim endure extreme pain without even flinching?

Is there a scientific explanation for his abilities, or is he truly unique?

In the world of marvels and wonders, few stories are as captivating as that of Tim Cridland. If you've ever accidentally stubbed your toe against a table leg, you know how even a tiny bit of pain can send you hopping around. Now, imagine a man who can push needles through his arms or swallow sharp swords without even a single wince of pain. Sounds impossible, right? Meet Tim Cridland, often known as "Zamora the Torture King."

Born in a world where superheroes graced the pages of comic books and screens of movie theaters, Tim seemed to have stepped out of one of those fantastical stories. However, instead of a cape, his superpower was an incredible resistance to pain.

Tim's journey into the world of pain began when he was relatively young. Intrigued by the ancient practices of body piercing and rituals in various cultures, he started experimenting on himself. Before anyone knew it, Tim was showcasing acts that would make even the toughest person squirm in their seat.

But here's the thing: while most of us would cringe at the very thought of such acts, for Tim, it was as simple as biting into a sandwich. In front of wide-eyed audiences, he would calmly push skewers through his body, walk on burning embers, and perform acts that seemed downright impossible.

As word of Tim's hair-raising stunts spread, people from all over flocked to see the "Torture King" in action. Newspapers wrote about him, TV shows featured his acts, and kids swapped stories of his seemingly superhuman feats on school playgrounds.

Many assumed it was a trick, perhaps some cleverly concealed protective gear or distraction technique. But scientists and doctors who examined him couldn't find any deception. They did, however, stumble upon something intriguing. Tests revealed that Tim's pain threshold was significantly higher than the average person's. But why? Was he born this way? Or did he train his body and mind over the years?

Amidst all the speculation and wonder, Tim continued to push boundaries. With every act, every performance, he seemed to be challenging the very limits of the human body and spirit, leaving audiences everywhere both horrified and utterly fascinated.

As the years went by, Tim's variety of daredevil acts expanded. Beyond the skewers and fire-walking, he started to introduce more complex and even dangerous performances. He'd lie on beds of nails, hang heavy weights from pierced parts of his body, and on some occasions, he even swallowed flaming torches. It was as if he was on a quest to redefine the boundaries of what the human body could endure.

But Tim's acts were not just about showcasing his resistance to pain. In many interviews, he spoke about the deeper, spiritual side to what he did. For Tim, it wasn't just about showing off or scaring people. It was about connecting with age-old traditions and rituals from different cultures. Many ancient civilizations had rites of passage that involved enduring pain to symbolize strength, resilience, or spiritual awakening. Tim saw himself as a modern-day representative of these ancient rituals, reintroducing them to a world that had long forgotten their significance.

However, with the rising popularity also came skepticism. Many medical professionals were intrigued by Tim's abilities. They wanted to know if this was a psychological phenomenon or if there was something biologically different about him. Some experts believed that Tim had mastered the art of meditation and mindfulness to such an extent that he could mentally "switch off" pain. Others thought that his frequent exposure to pain might have altered the way his nerve endings responded.

Intriguingly, Tim always remained somewhat elusive about his "secret." He often mentioned that it was a combination of mental training, understanding his body, and embracing the pain. But he never gave away too much, adding to the enigma surrounding him.

Offstage, away from the glaring lights and the gasping audiences, Tim Cridland was a much more private individual. Those close to him spoke of a deeply introspective man, someone who constantly questioned the world around him and his place in it. For Tim, the acts were not just about defying pain but about understanding oneself, challenging personal boundaries, and discovering inner strength.

As we wrap up the tale of the enigmatic "Torture King," the mysteries linger. How did he manage those incredible feats? Was it sheer willpower, a unique body physiology, or a deep spiritual understanding? Perhaps it's a blend of all these factors. But one thing is for sure: Tim Cridland's story reminds us of the astonishing potentials of the human body and spirit, pushing us to question our own boundaries and what we're capable of.

Mehran Karimi Nasseri

How could a man live in an airport for almost
18 years without ever taking a flight?

What circumstances led to Mehran Karimi
Nasseri's extended airport stay, and why
couldn't he leave?

Airports are places of comings and goings. Every day, countless people rush through their terminals, heading off to new adventures or returning home. But for Mehran Karimi Nasseri, an airport in Paris became his home for a very, very long time.

Born in Iran, Nasseri's life was not always tied to airport terminals. As a young man, he pursued his studies in the UK and lived a relatively normal life. But political tensions back in his home country changed everything. When Nasseri spoke out against the Iranian government, it landed him in some deep trouble. Fearing for his safety, he made the tough choice to seek refuge in another country.

After a series of complications, Nasseri found himself at the Charles de Gaulle Airport in Paris in 1988. His intention was never to stay, but a peculiar twist of fate would change that. You see, while waiting for a flight to the UK, he claimed that his passport and refugee documents were stolen. Without these crucial papers, he was in a legal limbo. The UK wouldn't accept him without his refugee status documents, and France couldn't just send him back to Iran, where he was in danger.

So what was Nasseri to do? With no immediate solution, days at the airport turned into weeks, then months, and astonishingly, years!

The bustling airport became Nasseri's universe. He made a home in the departure lounge, with its shiny floors, rows of seats, and the constant hum of

175

announcements overhead. People might find it hard to believe, but he managed to create a routine for himself. He read newspapers, wrote in his diary, and watched the waves of passengers, each absorbed in their own journey, mostly unaware of his unique plight.

Though many of us might think of airports as uncomfortable places for extended stays, Nasseri seemed to adapt. He became a fixture at Terminal 1, so much so that he earned the nickname "Sir Alfred" among airport staff and frequent travelers. They would often stop by for a chat, bringing him food and sometimes gifts. His unusual residency even drew media attention from around the world.

It's bizarre to think about, isn't it? While most of us can't wait to leave an airport after a long flight, Nasseri seemed content in his little corner of Charles de Gaulle. But as the years went by, the question on everyone's mind was: would Mehran Karimi Nasseri ever leave the airport and find a place to truly call home? And how could such a situation even be allowed to persist for so long?

You'd think living in an airport would become unbearably repetitive, right? But for Nasseri, every day brought its own set of adventures. Sometimes journalists would visit, eager to hear his story. Other times, curious travelers would strike up a conversation, making his day a bit brighter. But it wasn't always easy. The nights were often cold, and the constant noise of the airport made sleeping a challenge.

Yet, Nasseri's unique situation began to intrigue filmmakers and writers. His life inspired movies and books, with actors portraying his extraordinary airport life. As the years went on, Nasseri became more than just "the man at the airport"; he became a symbol of resilience and the human spirit's ability to adapt.

Still, everyone hoped for a resolution. Over the years, lawyers and human rights advocates tried to find a solution to Nasseri's situation. It was a complex puzzle: how do you help someone who has no official documents and can't legally live in any country?

Finally, after almost 18 years in 2006, a breakthrough came. French authorities granted Nasseri permission to live in France, but there was a catch. Even though he was now free to leave the airport and live in the country, he had become so accustomed to his airport life that the idea of leaving was daunting. It was all he had known for nearly two decades.

Eventually, with the help of those who cared about him, Nasseri did step outside the airport's sliding doors. He entered a world that had changed so much since he first arrived at Charles de Gaulle. The skyscrapers were taller, the cars were different, and the world outside moved at a pace he wasn't used to.

Nasseri's story reminds us that home isn't just a place; it's a feeling. It's proof that even in the strangest of circumstances, we can find a sense of belonging. So, next time you're at an airport, waiting for a flight, and feeling a little impatient, think of Nasseri and how he turned a waiting area into a world of its own.

CARLOS KAISER

How did Carlos Kaiser manage to get signed
by top soccer clubs without ever playing a
match?

Was Kaiser a genius manipulator, or were
soccer clubs too trusting?

In the world of soccer, there are superstar players known for their incredible skills, scoring goals, and leading their teams to victory. And then, there's Carlos Kaiser. If you were to look up his stats, you wouldn't find records of goals scored or memorable matches. Instead, you'd discover a web of tales about a man who had the boldness to fake an entire professional soccer career!

Born Carlos Henrique Raposo in 1963 in Rio de Janeiro, Brazil, Kaiser dreamed of the glamour that came with being a professional soccer player. The roaring crowds, the fame, the fortune... who wouldn't want a piece of that? But there was just one tiny problem: Kaiser wasn't very good at soccer. So, how did he become one of the most talked-about players without ever really playing?

At the heart of Kaiser's "career" were his unparalleled charm and cunning. He knew just how to weave stories, name-drop famous players, and present himself with enough swagger to convince clubs of his supposed talents. One of his most common tactics? Faking injuries.

In the mid-1980s, Kaiser managed to sign a contract with Botafogo, a top-tier team in Brazil. On his very first day of training, with new teammates curious to see their latest addition, Kaiser knew he needed an escape plan.

As the players began to kick the ball around, Kaiser started to sprint towards it. But before anyone could see his skills (or lack thereof), he suddenly collapsed, clutching his leg and crying out in pain. Everyone rushed

179

towards him, concerned for their new teammate. Kaiser was carried off the field, grimacing in pain. He told the coach that he had pulled a muscle and might be out of action for a while.

Weeks turned into months. While the team practiced, Kaiser would be on the sidelines, cheering them on, providing "strategic" advice, or pretending to receive treatment for his "injury." He kept this up for the entire duration of his contract!

During his time at Botafogo, he never played a single match, but he was always around, sharing tales of his (made-up) experiences with top European clubs and giving interviews about his recovery. The best part? He was getting paid for all of it!

This story might sound unbelievable, but it was just one chapter in the bizarre journey of Carlos Kaiser. Over the years, he'd repeat variations of this tactic with different clubs, always managing to escape just before being found out.

Carlos Kaiser's tale is not just about the audacity of one man, but also about the world of soccer in the 1980s and 1990s, where fact-checking wasn't as rigorous as it is today. Kaiser wasn't a football legend in the traditional sense, but he surely was legendary for pulling off one of the greatest cons in sports history.

While many saw Kaiser's antics as devious and cunning, there were those who were genuinely enchanted by his charisma. His infectious personality and the way he told his tales made even some skeptics turn into believers.

To maintain the façade, Carlos surrounded himself with actual soccer players and celebrities. He'd show up at parties with renowned footballers, ensuring he was always seen in the right circles. His connections played a crucial part in his deception, lending more credibility to his tales. If he was always with soccer stars, he had to be one himself, right?

But not all of his acts were just about maintaining the ruse. Some of them bordered on the brilliant. There's the tale of when he was almost caught during a training session. Instead of actually joining the practice, Kaiser would often tie his shoelaces or chat with spectators. One day, a coach insisted that he join in. Thinking on his feet, Kaiser deliberately kicked the ball into the stands. He then spent the rest of the session fetching balls, avoiding any real participation.

Kaiser's mastery over manipulation wasn't just limited to coaches and teams. He also managed to fool the media. He would give interviews, talking about his football career in Europe, using names of real clubs and players, adding twists to real stories he had heard, making them his own. With no internet to fact-check his claims instantly, many journalists took his words at face value.

His luck, however, couldn't last forever. As the years went by and as technology and media became more intrusive, it became harder and harder for Kaiser to keep up the act. His scams started to unravel. Players from teams he claimed to have played for began calling out his lies. Journalists started piecing together the fact that there wasn't a single piece of footage of Kaiser playing a professional match.

Yet, even when confronted with the truth, Kaiser never lost his charm. He'd laugh off accusations, shift the conversation, or come up with another unbelievable story. He wasn't just dodging tackles on the field; he was dodging the truth at every turn!

In many ways, Carlos Kaiser represents the lengths to which people will go to live a dream. His is a tale not of soccer prowess but of audacious imagination, unmatched confidence, and the human desire to be someone else, even if just for a little while.

Today, Kaiser's legend continues to grow. While he never scored a goal, he certainly made a mark. He's often invited to soccer events, podcasts, and interviews, where he laughs about his past, winking at the world that was once entirely fooled by him.

While the world of soccer has seen many greats — Pelé, Maradona, Messi — there will only ever be one Carlos Kaiser: the man who played soccer without ever really playing.

FRANK ABAGNALE JR.

Was Frank Abagnale Jr. truly just a genius con
artist, or was there more to his story?

How did a teenager manage to outsmart some
of the world's best security systems and
professionals?

Bef{}ore identity theft was a phrase you'd hear about on the news, and long before the age of social media profiles and online scams, there was a young man named Frank Abagnale Jr. And let's be clear: Frank was not your typical teenager.

When most teens were worrying about school dances or getting their driver's licenses, Frank was pulling off some of the most daring cons and heists the world had ever seen. One of his most jaw-dropping acts? Posing as a Pan American World Airways pilot and flying all around the world. For free.

Yeah, you read that right.

The year was 1964, and Frank was just 16 when he figured out the magic of an airline pilot's uniform. To most people, it screamed authority, trust, and, perhaps most importantly, free travel. With nothing but a fake pilot's license and a whole lot of courage, Frank managed to hitch rides on over 250 flights, spanning 26 countries, all without ever touching the controls of a plane.

Here's how it went down: Frank, ever observant, noticed how airline crews would often hop on flights for free, a perk offered to employees. With that knowledge, he devised a plan. He got himself a pilot's uniform by calling Pan Am's headquarters, pretending to be a pilot who had lost his uniform, and asked where he could get a replacement. They, believing his story, directed him to a company store where he obtained one. Then, using a toy security badge-making kit and some borrowed Pan

Am logos, he crafted himself a somewhat convincing pilot's ID.

Now, equipped with his uniform and ID, he would show up at airports, confidently strut to the jump seat (a seat for off-duty pilots) in the cockpit, and fly to his next destination. Pilots and crews just assumed he was a young pilot being moved from one place to another. Frank had become an expert at exploiting the trust people put in uniforms and titles.

During these flights, he'd chat with the crew, asking questions and gleaning little bits of information he'd later use to refine his act. To finance his escapades, he'd cash fake payroll checks from Pan Am at various banks.

His confidence and attention to detail were so good that no one suspected he was just a teenager pretending to be someone else. But, as with all things, there were moments where he almost got caught. Like the time he was "assigned" to a flight crew for a few days and they began to suspect something was off. Frank quickly made an excuse and disappeared before anyone could confront him.

The dreamlike life of posing as a pilot was thrilling, but Frank's adventures didn't stop in the sky. His boldness knew no bounds, and soon, he donned a different kind of suit—one that would make him a "doctor." With the same ease he had faked flying, Frank landed a position as a supervising resident of a hospital in Georgia, all without a proper medical degree. He relied on his charm, his ability to learn quickly, and the trusty tactic of always referring to the actual doctors for the real medical decisions.

But even as Frank walked the hospital halls with a stethoscope around his neck, he knew this wasn't a game he could play forever. The stakes were high, and the consequences of being caught were becoming very real. Every day brought a new risk of exposure, and with every close call, Frank's pulse raced just a little faster.

His journey took another twist when he transformed into a "lawyer." With an impressive forged Harvard transcript, Frank passed the bar exam in Louisiana and landed a job in the state attorney's office. He was living a life that was stranger than fiction, juggling identities like a circus performer, and always staying one step ahead of the law.

Yet, as the saying goes, all good things must come to an end. Frank's escapades eventually caught up with him when an Air France attendant recognized his face from a wanted poster. Before he knew it, Frank's world of make-believe crumbled around him, and he found himself behind bars in France, then later in Sweden, and finally sent back to the United States.

The once carefree teenager who had flown to exotic destinations and walked into any room with unearned authority was now a prisoner, wearing handcuffs instead of pilot wings. It was in the quiet of his cell that Frank had time to think about his whirlwind adventures—the risks, the excitement, and the inevitable fall.

But Frank's story doesn't end with a life behind bars. In a twist of fate, the FBI recognized his talent and offered him a deal: help them catch other forgers and teach them about the tricks of the trade, and he could walk free. Frank agreed, and thus began the next chapter of his life, working as a consultant for the very people who had worked so tirelessly to catch him.

In the years that followed, Frank Abagnale Jr. became a leading expert in fraud prevention, using his past misdeeds to help protect others from the kind of life he once led. He wrote books, gave lectures, and even had his story turned into a hit movie, showing that redemption is possible, no matter how twisted the path.

Frank's journey from a teenage con artist to a respected authority on security is a testament to the power of change and the possibility that within every wrongdoer lies the potential for good. For the teens reading his story, Frank Abagnale Jr. serves as a tale of the dangers of deception but also as an inspiring example of how one can turn their life around and fly right—even without a pilot's license.

AFTERWORD

Bravo, young investigator! As we turn the last page of *History's Mysterious People,* I hope you've found our voyage as thrilling and captivating as I have! Together, we've traveled the world, exploring the lives of curious figures and unraveling the mysteries they left behind.

Remember our journey to the mystical realms of Tibetan Tummo Monks and the strange sleeplessness of Ngoc Thai? We' delved into the fascinating abilities of Wolf Messing and pondered the astonishing appetite of Tarrare.

Our quest also took us to explore the enigmatic life of Fulcanelli, and we stood in wonder at the insights and mysterious life of Edgar Cayce. And the curious case of the stranded traveler Mehran Karimi Nasseri and the intriguing life of master impostor Frank Abagnale Jr. added layers of adventure to our exploration.

We've ventured through the captivating tales of Kevin Richardson's unique bond with lions and Wim Hof's extraordinary feats against extreme cold. The bizarre yet true story of Tim Cridland and his remarkable tolerance for pain left us astounded, as did the journey into the life of the psychic spy Joseph McMoneagle.

Each figure has been a tribute to the endless wonders and mysteries that humanity holds. As we part ways, I hope this journey has ignited a lifelong flame of curiosity and exploration within you.

With the world as a canvas of endless mysteries, remember that it's filled with infinite questions and boundless discoveries. So, keep exploring, keep questioning, and above all, keep marveling at the world around you!

Farewell for now, young explorers, until our paths cross again in the next great adventure. The future is brimming with possibilities, and I eagerly await the discoveries your curiosity will unearth next. Until then, keep the spirit of discovery with you.

Happy exploring!
Arch Stanton

Star Odyssey Press